The Poetry of Motion

Books by Alan Bold

Poetry
Society Inebrious
The Voyage
To Find the New
A Perpetual Motion Machine
Penguin Modern Poets 15 (with Morgan and Brathwaite)
The State of the Nation
The Auld Symie
He will be Greatly Missed
A Century of People
A Pint of Bitter
Scotland, Yes
This Fine Day
A Celtic Quintet (with Bellamy)
In This Corner: Selected Poems 1963—83
Stories
Hammer and Thistle (with Morrison)
Criticism
Thom Gunn & Ted Hughes
George Mackay Brown
The Ballad
(ed.) *Smollett: Author of the First Distinction*
(ed.) *The Sexual Dimension in Literature*
The Sensual Scot
Modern Scottish Literature
MacDiarmid: The Terrible Crystal
(ed.) *Scott: The Long-Forgotten Melody*
(ed.) *Byron: Wrath and Rhyme*
Anthologies
The Penguin Book of Socialist Verse
The Martial Muse: Seven Centuries of War Poetry
The Cambridge Book of English Verse 1939—75
Making Love: The Picador Book of Erotic Verse
The Bawdy Beautiful: The Sphere Book of Improper Verse
Mounts of Venus: The Picador Book of Erotic Prose
Drink to Me Only: The Prose (and Cons) of Drinking
A Scottish Poetry Book

The
Poetry of Motion

An Anthology of Sporting Verse
edited by Alan Bold

MAINSTREAM PUBLISHING   EDINBURGH

Copyright © The individual contributors
Introduction and selection © Alan Bold

First Published in Great Britain by
MAINSTREAM PUBLISHING COMPANY (EDINBURGH) LTD.
7 Albany Street
Edinburgh EH1 3UG

ISBN 0 906391 70 9

The publisher gratefully acknowledges the financial assistance of the Scottish Arts Council in the publication of this volume.

All rights reserved. No part of this book may be reproduced or transmitted in any form or by any means, mechanical or electric, including photocopy, recording or any information storage and retrieval system now know or to be invented, without permission from the publisher, except by a reviewer who wishes to quote brief passages in connexion with a review written for insertion in a magazine, newspaper or broadcast.

Typeset by Wayside Graphics, Clevedon, Avon
Printed in Great Britain by Forsyth Middleton

Contents

Introduction

Allan Ramsay (1685–1758)
  On the Royal Company of Archers   1

Rev Emanuel Collins (18th century)
  Epitaph   7

James Love (1722–74)
  Cricket   9

Anonymous (18th century)
  Bowling   10

James Grahame (1765–1811)
  from '*British Georgics*'   17

James Hogg (1770–1835)
  The Channel Stane   18

Anonymous (1782)
  The Tennis Court   19

Anonymous (1792)
  'To box or not to box'   20

William Wordsworth (1770–1850)
  from '*The Prelude*'   21

Samuel Taylor Coleridge (1772–1834)
  Lines Composed While Climbing   22

Frederick Lawson (19th century)
  Chaunt for Tom Cribb   23

Bob Gregson (1778–1824)
  British Lads and Black Millers   25

Thomas Moore (1779–1852)
  Epistle From Tom Cribb to Big Ben   26

Anonymous (19th century)
  Crib and the Black   28

Tom Hazel (19th century)
  Multum in Parvo   29

Anonymous (19th century)
  'Pray, havn't you heard'   30
  A-Boxing We Will Go   31
  Monody on the Death of Dick Curtis   32
  Heroic Stanzas from Bendigo to Deaf Burke   34
  The Unfinished Fight of the American Giant and the Tipton Slasher   36

Valentine from Bendigo to Brassey	38
An Heroic Epistle from Brassey to Big Caunt	39
The Combat of Sayerius and Heenanus	40
Chaunt for Tom Sayers	46

George Gordon, Lord Byron (1788–1824)
Written After Swimming from Sestos to Abydos	47
from '*The Two Foscari*'	47

Felicia Hemans (1793–1835)
The Diver	48

J. H. Reynolds (1794–1852)
None But Himself Can Be His Parallel	50
To John Randall, the Famous Pugilist	50
What is Life?	51
Song (from *King Timms-the First*)	53
Lines to Philip Samson	54
from '*The Fields of Tothill*'	55

John Keats (1795–1821)
Written Upon the Top of Ben Nevis	56

Anonymous (19th century)
The Currie Curlers	56
The Curler's Complaint	58

George Murray (1812–81)
The Broom and Channel-Stane	59

Anonymous (19th century)
The Game of Cricket	59

Walt Whitman (1819–92)
The Runner	60

Lewis Carroll (1832–98)
The Deserted Parks (Oxford)	61

Anonymous (19th century)
The Football Match	61

Algernon Charles Swinburne (1837–1909)
A Swimmer's Dream	62

Andrew Lang (1844–1912)
Brahma	65
A Song of Life and Golf	66
Ballade of Cricket	67
Ballade of Dead Cricketers	67
Ballade of the Three Graces	68
A Ballade of Mourning	69

James Kennedy (1848–1922)
Elegy on the Death of James Fleming	70
The Curler	72
The Quoit Players	74

G. F. Grace (1850–80)
    The Lost Ball   78

Robert Louis Stevenson (1850–94)
    The Canoe Speaks   79

William Henry Drummond (1854–1907)
    The Great Fight   80

Edward Cracroft Lewfroy (1855–91)
    A Cricket-Bowler   83
    A Football-Player   83

William Sharp (1855–1905)
    The Swimmer of Nemi   84
    The Bather   84

Arthur Conan Doyle (1859–1930)
    A Reminiscence of Cricket   86

A. E. Housman (1859–1936)
    To an Athlete Dying Young   88

J. K. Stephen (1859–92)
    Boating Song   89
    The Hundred Yards Race   91
    Parker's Piece, May 19, 1891   92

Francis Thompson (1859–1907)
    At Lord's   93

Sir Henry Newbolt (1862–1938)
    Vitaï Lampada   94

W. B. Yeats (1865–1939)
    At Galway Races   95

Stephen Crane (1871–1900)
    'I saw a man pursuing the horizon'   96

Robert Service (1874–1958)
    The Bruiser   96

John Masefield (1878–1967)
    The Racer   97

Alfred Noyes (1880–1958)
    The Swimmer's Race   98

P. G. Wodehouse (1881–1975)
    Missed!   99

William Carlos Williams (1883–1963)
    At the Ball Game   100

J. C. Squire (1884–1958)
    The Rugger Match   102

Ezra Pound (1885–1972)
    For E. McC   109

Siegfried Sassoon (1886–1967)
    The Extra Inch   110

Eugene O'Neill (1888–1953)
    'I used to ponder deeply'   110

Hugh MacDiarmid (1892–1978)
    from '*The Kind of Poetry I Want*'
    Glasgow, 1960   111

Charles Hamilton Sorley (1895–1915)
    The Song of the Ungirt Runners   113

F. Scott Fitzgerald (1896–1940)
    Football   114

F. R. Higgins (1896–1941)
    The Old Jockey   115

Hart Crane (1899–1932)
    The Bathers   115

Sir John Betjeman (1906–1984)
    Seaside Golf   116

Louis MacNeice (1907–63)
    The Cyclist   117

John Pudney (1909–77)
    The Speed Boat   118

Bernard Spencer (1909–63)
    Table-Tennis   118

Norman MacCaig (born 1910)
    Highland Games   119

Kenneth Allott (1912–73)
    Lament for a Cricket Eleven   120

John Arlott (born 1914)
    Cricket at Worcester, 1938   121

Norman Nicholson (born 1914)
    Old Man at a Cricket Match   122

Betty Parvin (born 1916)
    The Hockey Field   123

Gavin Ewart (born 1916)
    September Cricket, 1975   124

Jake Willis (born 1917)
    Mighty Mouse   125

John Jarvis (born 1917)
    'The Hurricane'   126

Walker Gibson (born 1919)
    Billiards   127

Vernon Scannell (born 1922)
    Mastering the Craft   128

Alan Ross (born 1922)
    Cricket at Brighton   129
    Stanley Matthews   130
    World Cup   131

Dannie Abse (born 1923)
    The Game   132

James Kirkup (born 1923)
    Rugby League Game   133

Michael Ivens (born 1924)
    Sparrow at Lords Museum   134

John Smith (born 1924)
    Advice to Swimmers   134

Philip Booth (born 1925)
    First Lesson   135

Kenneth Koch (born 1925)
    from *'Ko, or A Season on Earth'*   136

Maxine Kumin (born 1925)
    400-Meter Freestyle   145

Alistair Mackie (born 1925)
    Drappit   146
    Don't cry for Argentina for me   147

Christopher Logue (born 1926)
    Mohammed Ali   147

Charles Tomlinson (born 1927)
    Swimming Chenango Lake   148

Philip Oakes (born 1928)
    Death of the Referee   149

Iain Crichton Smith (born 1928)
    School Sports and the Turnistiles   150

Colin Shakespeare (born 1929)
    To Sir Len Hutton on his 65th Birthday   150

Tony Connor (born 1930)
    In the Locker Room   151

Ted Hughes (born 1930)
    Football at Slack   151

Martin Green (born 1932)
    Ode to Hackney Marshes   152

Adrian Mitchell (born 1932)
    World Cup Song   153

J. M. Anthony (born 1934)
    The Last Over   154

Stephen Morris (born 1935)
    High Jump Poem   155
    Long Jump Poem   156

Jeff Cloves (born 1937)
    Tonight I feel like a basketball hero   157
    beryl and her bike   157
    Fanny Blankers-Koen at Wembley   158
    For Fausto Coppi (1916–60)   158
    wonder boy   159
    the slow bowler's curve   160

Michael Horovitz (born 1935)
    The Game   161

Roger McGough (born 1937)
    40–Love   164

Susan Wilkins (born 1938)
    Running Sequence   165

Anonymous (20th century)
    The High Jump   166

Caroline Ackroyd (born 1939)
    Prizewinner   167

Donald Campbell (born 1940)
    Tynecastle   167

Robert Hughes (born 1940)
    The Races   168

Pat Cutts (born 1941)
    Kitchen Conversation   168

David Morrison (born 1941)
    Jacqueline (Badminton)   169

Stephen Vincent (born 1941)
    Basketball   169

Bill Costley (born 1942)
    'The Smiler With The Knife'   170

Douglas Dunn (born 1942)
    Runners   170
    'In ten seconds'   171

Muhammad Ali (born 1942)
    The Greatest   171
    Feats of Clay   172

Oscar Bonavena	172
Joe Frazier	173
The Ali–Foreman Fight	173

Dave Smith (born 1942)
Blues for Benny Kid Paret	174

Alan Bold (born 1943)
Game and Match	175
Kenny Dalglish	175
Archie Gemmill	176
The Swimmer	177
The Cyclist	177

Bruce Davies (born 1943)
The Rubgy Match	178

Tom Leonard (born 1944)
Yon Night	179
Fireworks	180
from *'Unrelated Incidents'*	180

Danny Pollock (born 1944)
Goakeeper's Lament	181
Dart Board Dave	182

Peter Bond (born 1945)
Pockets of Resistance	183

Martin Hall (born 1945)
I'll Stand the Lot of You	183

John Whitworth (born 1945)
Sporting Prints	184
Slow Left Arm	185

Peter Forbes (born 1947)
Cricket	185
Building an Innings	186

Alan Frost (born 1947)
Goal!	186
Car	187

Ron Butlin (born 1949)
Football Fantasy: Argentina 1978	188

Christopher Reid (born 1949)
Folk Tale	190
Baldanders	190

Carlton C. Allen (born 1954)
Wimbledon Wizard	191
Platinum Ballerina	192

F. Scott Monument (born 1956)
The Keepfit Fiend	193

The Dartist	193
The Angler	194
The Hillwalker	194
The Golf Freak	194
Acknowledgements	196
Glossary	199
Index of Poets	200

Introduction

Though the public is accustomed to accepting a synthesis of aesthetics and athletics in the cinema – as witness the artistry involved in the great American boxing films, culminating in Sylvester Stallone's magnificent *Rocky* triptych – there is a furtive fallacy about poetry dealing exclusively with metaphysical rather than physical matters. When (or if) the general public thinks of poetry it automatically recalls images from schooldays when the poet was presented as an effete individual pursuing impossibly unworldly ideals. Since few people retain an interest in poetry after learning to detest the subject at school, the impression remains of the poet as pansy or duffer or weirdo or eedjit. The aesthete and the athlete are held to be extremes incapable of meeting. As Norman Mailer put it, in *The Fight* (1976), 'For Ali to compose a few words of real poetry would be equal to an intellectual throwing a good punch.' The implications are obvious – and completely misleading.

In *A Literature of Sports* (1980) Tom Hodge refers to 'one of the reasons why more young people are interested in sports than in poetry: societies almost always reward aggressive rather than passive behaviour, especially among males'. Actually the world of poetry is a highly competitive place in which participants struggle against each other for prestige instead of prize money. Such an activity is regarded as odd in an economy that worships the profit and avoids the prophet. Poetry is seen as something eccentric, something unmanly and unwholesome and it must be admitted that the non-athletic connotations of poetry have been reinforced by the poor physical health of some of the century's most visible poets. The sight of a poet – like Robert Graves – stripped for action is surprising enough to cause comment. Dylan Thomas was something of a physical wreck who disintegrated so drastically that no hospital could have put all the pieces together again. Robert Lowell, though strong enough to pack a good punch (Norman Mailer, please note) in a fracas, had a frenzied wild-eyed institutional appearance to go with his confessional verse. Lowell's poem 'To Delmore Schwartz' cleverly conveys the non-athletic lifestyle favoured by some poets:

> We drank and eyed
> The chicken-hearted shadows of the world.
> Underseas fellows, nobly mad,
> we talked away our friends. 'Let Joyce and Freud,
> the Masters of Joy,
> be our guests here,' you said. The room was filled
> with cigarette smoke circling the paranoid,
> inert gaze of Coleridge, back
> from Malta – his eyes lost in flesh, lips baked and black.

The ambience evoked by Lowell aches with anxiety.

Because poetry is full of pathos it has been convenient to categorise poets as pathetic figures forever succumbing to solipsistic sickness. So many people need to see the world schematically (with Us opposing Them) that they welcome the notion of the split between body and mind. Athletes are supposed to be swift but stupid; artists clever but clumsy. The contrast has been an easy one to encourage, especially since Gilbert and Sullivan conjured up an unforgettably absurd aesthete in *Patience* (1881):

> A pallid and thin young man,
> A haggard and lank young man,
> A greenery-yellery, Grosvenor Gallery,
>   Foot-in-the-grave young man!

The physically feeble aesthete is always good for a laugh. Saul Bellow's *Humboldt's Gift* (1975) portrays the author's friend (in fiction Von Humboldt Fleisher, in fact the aforementioned Delmore Schwartz) sympathetically but also with a comic touch that reduces the poet to a figure of physical fun:

> Humboldt himself was just beginning to put on weight. He was thick through the shoulders but still narrow at the hips. Later he got a prominent belly, like Babe Ruth. His legs were restless and his feet made nervous movements. Below, shuffling comedy; above, princeliness and dignity, a certain nutty charm. A surfaced whale beside your boat might look at you as he looked with his wide-set grey eyes . . . His forehead was scarred. As a kid he had fallen on a skate blade, the bone itself was dented. His pale lips were prominent and his mouth was full of immature-looking teeth, like milk teeth. He consumed his cigarettes to the last spark and freckled his tie and his jacket with burns . . . Also, he was a pretty good drinker.

For all that I believe that inside every aesthete there's an athlete struggling to get out (and vice versa since the two activities have in common a celebration of grace and endurance). Aestheticism is a protective pose to disguise insecurity, and poetic outfits and attitudes are peripheral paraphernalia. Almost every human activity has a suitable mode of dress; just as team players wear uniforms so poets have evolved what they consider to be an appropriate sartorial style. Dress, however, is optional and the poet can perform just as well whether dressed as a bank clerk (like Eliot) or a lifeguard (like Graves). So when we consider art and sport closely it should come as no surprise to find that poets enthusiastically applaud athletic effort even if few of them are equipped to participate competently in athletic events. It is not difficult to understand why the aesthete admires the athlete. There is a rhythm and physical fluency in sport that lifts the gifted individual beyond the limitations that keep the rest of us firmly on the ground. What the poet achieves by the exercise of his (or her) imagination the athlete embodies in himself (or herself). The great athlete, it has often been observed, is poetry in motion. To watch the sporting virtuoso in action – Ali in the ring, say, or Pele on the soccer pitch – is to witness a rare muscular vision. For the great athlete does not only act instinctively; he considers the implications of every move and anticipates the response to it. Pele could 'read' a situation in football superbly. Similarly, Ali told Norman Mailer after he (Ali, that is, though Mailer did his bit vicariously) had won back the World Heavyweight title from George Foreman that his approach was, above all, thoughtful: 'Maybe they'll admit that now I am the professor of boxing.' Coincidentally, Ali's preparation for that fight had included sessions with the muscular muse (as Mailer observed):

The poem [Ali read] had been three pages. 'How long did it take to write?' he was asked. 'Five hours,' he replied – Ali who could talk at the rate of three hundred new words a minute. Since the respect was for the man, for all of the man . . . so came an image of Ali, pencil in hand, composing down there in the depths of Black reverence for rhyme – those mysterious links in the universe of sound: no rhyme ever without its occult reason . . . Ali's psychic powers were never long removed, however, from any critical situation. 'That stuff,' he said, waving his hands, 'is just for fun. I got serious poetry I'm applying my mind to.' He looked interested for the first time this day in what he was doing.

There are other examples of athletes writing verse (Bob Gregson, for example) and the reverence of a man like Ali for poetry suggests that art is the condition the athlete aspires to as he sees his skill transcending technique and affirming a vision. The fact that Ali's boxing exploits are (or were) vastly superior to his poems is a result of personal circumstances and does not reinforce the either/or aesthete–athlete schism (as Mailer seems to think with his strangely snobbish contempt for Ali's literary attempts). After all, though Byron was a fine swimmer, Pound an adroit fencer, and Vernon Scannell a good boxer they are the exceptions to the rule which is that poets approach sport as spectators. Athletes, by the same process, approach art as amateurs. Art and sport are not mutually exclusive but each discipline is so demanding that it is almost impossible for excellence to be achieved in both by one person. What poets and athletes share is an appreciation of the quintessentially human quality of individual expression so it is worth remembering that even team games depend on unique players whose ingenuity disrupts a predictable routine. Acclaim, in sport and poetry, comes to those who avoid safety-first solutions and remake the world in their own image – or imagery. At the great moments of art and sport the individual achievement is caught in a timeless dimension that promises poetic immortality and keeps the athlete forever young. The great sporting poem, like the great sporting person, enhances humanity and inspires by example.

Sporting, or athletic, poetry can be defined as verse whose thematic movement suggests great physical effort or extraordinary muscular coordination. Boxing or football obviously require tremendous fitness; snooker or darts, by contrast, depend on subtle muscular movements. Angling verse, though, does not really affirm the spirit of sport because in that pursuit the athletic prowess is exhibited by the victim, not the victor. Taunting and killing a fish from a safe distance seems no more sporting than butchering a piece of dead meat. Byron put it well in *Don Juan* when he put angling in its proper place as a 'solitary vice':

> Then there were billiards; cards, too, but *no* dice; –
>   Save in the clubs no man of honour plays; –
> Boats when 'twas water, skating when 'twas ice,
>   And the hard frost destroy'd the scenting days:
> And angling, too, that solitary vice,
>   Whatever Izaak Walton sings or says:
> The quaint, old, cruel coxcomb, in his gullet
> Should have a hook, and a small trout to pull it.

The presence of Byron draws attention to the two types of sporting verse. First, there is the poetry produced by professional poets who use sport as a specific theme on which to play intricate variations. Randall Jarrell's 'Say Good-bye to Big Daddy' explores the tragic aspects of sport:

> Big Daddy, who found football easy enough, life hard enough
> To – after his last night cruising Baltimore
> In his yellow Cadillac – to die of heroin;
> Big Daddy, who was scared, he said: 'I've been scared
> Most of my life. You wouldn't think so to look at me.
> It gets so bad I cry myself to sleep –' his size
> Embarrassed him, so that he was helped by smaller men
> And hurt by smaller men; Big Daddy Lipscomb
> Has helped to his feet the last ball carrier, Death.

In a lower league than that there is the occasional verse turned out by amateurs anxious to record an event or eulogise a favourite. Such amateur verse often concentrates so literally on the subject that there is no room for any imaginative manoeuvre. For example, a ninety-three round bare-fisted prize-fight between Ben Caunt and William 'Bendigo' Thompson at Newport Pagnell on 9 September 1845 provoked, within a day or so, a broadside:

> And near to Newport Pagnell,
> Those men did strip so fine,
> Ben Caunt stood six foot two and a half,
> And Bendigo five foot nine,
> Ben Caunt a giant did appear,
> And made the claret flow,
> And he seemed fully determined
> Soon to conquer Bendigo.

And so it goes relentlessly on until Bendigo gets his disputed decision.

The commonplace phrases and rhymes of amateur verse are the metrical equivalents of the cliches of tabloid journalism. Nineteenth-century boxing broadsides will usually rhyme Tom Cribb's surname with fib and Ben Caunt's with (John of) Gaunt; in the same way headline writers have a whole repertoire of readymade puns and punchlines. Yet amateurism in verse should be no more despised than amateurism in sport. Metrical journalism is one of the last remaining links between the big public and the practice of poetry. Youngsters should be encouraged to rhyme out tributes to sporting heroes and fans of all ages should think of appropriate lines for the sport they have seen. If a middle-aged man is permitted a spot of Sunday soccer in the local park then the same tolerance should be extended to those who, now and then, want to indulge in a bit of rhyme. When more people write verse more will appreciate poetry as they will be in a position to distinguish between the workmanlike performance and the touch of genius. Poets everywhere, and at every level, should learn to mix with the crowd; at present too many literary people are afraid of being contaminated by contact with popular culture.

As critics like to determine what is permissible in verse, especially in an age when poetry is a minority art, sporting verse has been given little attention to date. Though they like to give an objective tone to their utterances the critics are almost always projecting their own prejudices and few of these concern sport. The aesthetic outlook of English critics is a rationalisation of attitudes deeply rooted in childhood and environment; indeed critical generalisations tell us more about the critic than the work under discussion. Critics tend to advocate a certain type of poetry – be it lyrical, narrative, confessional or mystical – because it expresses exactly the ideas they want to promote. F. R. Leavis's enthusiasm for edifying works of literature relates to his moralistic nature and A. Alvarez's ecstasy over confessional poetry is compatible with the suicidal obsessions he discloses in *The Savage God* (1971). I am not denying the value of criticism but pointing out that the critical ignorance about sporting verse is a consequence of literary strategy rather than what obtains artistically. When sport and athletic activities have an appeal for Byron, Keats, Yeats, Pound and Ted Hughes (to name but five) then it is as well to acknowledge that literary criticism has failed to take account of an area of enormous human and artistic interest. As I have dismissed the notion of absolute objectivity in criticism it is only fair play for me to declare a personal interest. Long before I was interested in poetry I was fascinated by sport. When I was a boy in Edinburgh I enrolled at the Sparta boxing club where I observed the astonishing prowess of another boy, Ken Buchanan, who eventually became Lightweight Champion of the world. Even as a kid, Ken had a devastatingly swift straight left and could confuse his opponents with the speed of his combinations. The rest of us watched him in awe, greatly appreciating his gifts. When he triumphed in the ring it was always with a stunning display of athletic artistry.

I was likewise fortunate in my early years in Edinburgh in being able to watch the Hibs team that won the Scottish League Championship in 1950–1 and 1951–2. With an attacking forward line comprising Smith–Johnstone–Reilly–Turnbull–Ormond the team delighted the fans with clever positional play and fast-moving manoeuvres. Subsequently I largely took it for granted that those who admired panache in poetry would also respond to it in sport, as the two phenomena sought their own kind of perfection. I also assumed that it was perfectly acceptable to write a book of football poems and, like everyone else in Scotland, anticipated a winning run in the World Cup to be held in Argentina that year. Prior to publication of my book *Scotland, Yes* (1978) there was a frontpage feature of some of my football poems in the Saturday literary section of *The Scotsman*. Immediately the newspaper was swamped with bitter letters complaining about the prominent display of football poems. Those who lined up acrimoniously against me claimed that poetry and sport were incompatible. Fortunately I was defended by Hugh MacDiarmid who realised (as do all great poets) that there is no such thing as an intrinsically poetic subject.

Poetry is not made by the subject itself but by the amount of imaginative pressure brought to bear on it. Some time before Eliot made poems out of the 'burnt-out ends of smoky days' there was a realisation that poetry could only survive by making itself more accessible and dropping some aristocratic affectations. Wordsworth's intention, as expressed in 1800 in the preface to *Lyrical Ballads*, was 'to choose incidents and situations from common life, and to relate or describe them, throughout, as far as was possible in a selection of language really used by men, and, at the same time, to throw over them a certain colouring of imagination, whereby ordinary things should be presented to the mind in an unusual aspect'. The debate Wordsworth initiated is still open and clearly poetry can flourish in two ways: ideally, the public can learn to live with great poetry; more realistically, poets can make some appeal to the public without abandoning their artistic integrity. When poets have the humanity to take an audience into account there is at least an opportunity of establishing a symbiotic relationship between poet and public. As the most memorable way of arranging words, poetry should be capable of embracing any subject at all and sport is especially attractive because of its ability to engage the emotions. Evidently many poets have enjoyed expressing themselves on sporting themes and I am sure that sporting verse has a splendid future to go with its glorious past.

If sport can provide poetry with a popular theme then poetry can, for its part, help to humanise sport by stressing its impact on the imagination. Journalists, and other prose-writers, often see sport in abstract terms, as a battle for the survival of the fittest. From this point of view athletes become symbols and personifications of power. Thus Ali versus Foreman becomes a conflict between the beautiful and the brutal while the Brazilian football team is invariably regarded as a collective force whose collective divinity is threatened by the Rest of the World. This approach is an extension of war-reporting. Just as William Howard Russell's reports to *The Times* from the Crimea are full of atmosphere and value judgements ('heroic countrymen rushing to the arms of death') so prose-writers inevitably see sport as a martial issue: the athletic arena becomes a military battlefield and the game is promoted as a regional or national conflict. Poets are able to see sport in a more meaningful way, as part of a grand human vision, because the poet values the individual not the abstraction; and because the poet has the insight to treat sport as an art.

For it is, ultimately, art that outlasts the injuries inflicted by time. It is poetry that preserves the motion. Thanks to J. H. Reynolds we can recall the flourish of the Fancy; thanks to Alan Ross's poem, Stanley Matthews will remain the wizard he was; thanks to Christopher Reid's metaphysical wit his golfer will go on gravitating towards his 'tiny, pock-marked planet'. Poetry and sport are both alive with the euphoria of being human. As Marianne Moore put it in 'Baseball and Writing':

Fanaticism? No. Writing is exciting
and baseball is like writing.
   You can never tell with either
     how it will go
     or what you will do;
   generating excitement –
   a fever in the victim –
   pitcher, catcher, fielder, batter.
     Victim in what category?
*Owl*man watching from the press box?
     to whom does it apply?
     who is excited? Might it be I?

Athletic effort has its own wordless eloquence but it is poetry that gives it such perfect definition. Examples abound hereafter and speak for themselves.

Alan Bold

Allan Ramsay
1685–1758

On the Royal Company of Archers shooting for the Bowl, July 6, 1724

On which Day his Grace James *Duke of* Hamilton *was chosen their Captain General; and* Mr. David Drummond *their Prieses won the Prize.*

Again the Year returns the Day,
That's dedicate to Joy and Play,
   To *Bonnets, Bows,* and *Wine.*
Let all who wear a sullen Face,
This Day meet with a due Disgrace,
   And in their sowrness pine;
Be shun'd as Serpents, that wad stang
   The Hand that gi'es them Food:
Sic we debar frae lasting Sang,
   And all their grumbling Brood.

While, to gain Sport and halesome Air,
The blythsome Spirit draps dull Care,
   And starts frae Bus'ness free.
Now to the Fields the *Archers* bend,
With friendly Minds the Day to spend,
   In manly Game and Glee;
First striving wha shall win the Bowl,
   And then gar't flow with Wine:
Sic manly Sport refresh'd the Soul
   Of stalwart Men lang syne.

E'er Parties thrawn, and Int'rest vile
Debauch'd the Grandeur of our Isle,
   And made ev'n Brethren Faes;
Syne Truth frae Friendship was exil'd,
And fause the honest Hearts beguil'd,
   And led them in a Maze
Of Politicks; – with cunning craft,
   The *Issachars* of State,
Frae haly Drums first dang us daft,
   Then drown'd us in Debate.

Drap this unpleasing Thought, dear Muse;
Come, view the Men thou likes to roose;
   To *Bruntsfield* Green let's hy,
And see the Royal *Bowmen* strive,
Wha far the feather'd Arrows drive,
   All soughing thro' the Sky;

Ilk ettling with his utmost Skill,
   With artfu' Draught and stark,
Exending Nerves with hearty Will,
   In hopes to hit the Mark.

See Hamilton, wha' moves with Grace,
Chief of the *Caledonian* Race
   Of Peers; to whom is due
All Honours, and a' fair renown;
Wha lays aside his Ducal Crown,
   Sometime to shade his Brow
Beneath St. *Andrew's* Bonnet blew,
   And joins to gain the Prize;
Which shaws true Merit match'd by few,
   Great, affable and wise.

This Day, with universal Voice,
The *Archers* Him their Chieftain chose,
   Consenting Powers divine,
They blest the Day with general Joy,
By giving him a princely Boy,
   To beautify his Line;
Whose Birth-day, in immortal Sang
   Shall stand in fair Record,
While bended Strings the *Archers* twang,
   And Beauty is ador'd.

Next Drummond view, who gives their Law;
It glads our Hearts to see him draw
   The Bow, and guide the *Band*;
He, like the Saul of a' the lave,
Does with sic Honour still behave,
   As merits to command.
Blyth be his Hours, hale be his Heart,
   And lang may he preside:
Lang the just Fame of his Desert
   Shall unborn *Archers* read.

How on this fair propitious Day,
With Conquest leal he bore away
   The Bowl victoriously;
With following Shafts in Number four,
Success the like ne'er ken'd before,
   The Prize to dignify.
Haste to the Garden then bedeen,
   The Rose and Laurel pow,
And plet a Wreath of white and green,
   To busk the Victor's Brow.

The Victor crown, who with his Bow,
In spring of Youth and am'rous Glow,
   Just fifty Years sinsyne,
The Silver Arrow made his Prize,
Yet ceases not in Fame to rise,
   And with new Feats to shine.
May every Archer strive to fill,
   His Bonnet, and observe,
The Pattern he has set with skill,
   And Praise like him deserve.

Rev. Emanuel Collins

18th century

Epitaph

Skidmore, a bruiser of renown,
Dreaded by bruisers in and out of town,
From a much greater bruiser met his fate,
By Death the bruiser was most soundly beat;
When Death and Skidmore first began to box,
Death gave to Skidmore most tremendous knocks,
And all throughout this most unequal battle,
Death made poor Skidmore's flesh and bones rattle;
Skidmore tried hardly to recover breath,
But was at last obliged to yield to Death.
Learn hence, ye who this bloody art have used,
By Death, the bruiser, you must all be bruised.

James Love
1722–74

Cricket*

BOOK I

The Argument of the First Book. – The Subject. Address to the Patron of Cricket. A Description of the Pleasures felt at the Approach of the proper Season for Cricket, and the Preparations for it. A Comparison between this game and others, particularly Billiards, Bowls, and Tennis. Exhortation to Britain to leave all meaner sports, and cultivate Cricket only, as most adapted to the Freedom and Hardiness of its Constitution. The Counties most famous for Cricket are describ'd, as vying with one another for Excellency.

  While others soaring on a lofty Wing,
Of dire *Bellona's* cruel Triumphs sing;
Sound the shrill Clarion, mount the rapid Car,
And rush delighted thro' the Ranks of War;
My tender Muse, in humbler, milder Strains,
Presents a bloodless Conquest on the Plains;
Where vig'rous Youth, in Life's fresh Bloom resort,
For pleasing Exercise and healthful Sport.
Where Emulation fires, where Glory draws,
And active Sportsmen struggle for Applause;
Expert to *Bowl,* to *Run,* to *Stop,* to Throw,
Each Nerve collected at each mighty Blow.

  Hail Cricket! glorious, manly, *British* game!
First of all Sports! be first alike in Fame!
To my fir'd Soul thy busy Transports bring,
That I may feel thy Raptures, while I sing!
And thou, kind Patron of the mirthful Fray,
Sandwich, thy Country's Friend, accept the Lay!
Tho' mean my Verse, my Subject yet approve,
And look propitious on the Game you love!

  When the returning Sun begins to smile,
And shed its Glories round this sea girt Isle;
When a new-born Nature deck'd in vivid Green,
Chaces dull Winter from the charming Scene:
High panting with Delight, the jovial Swain
Trips it exulting o'er the Flow'r-strew'd Plain;
Thy Pleasures, Cricket! all his Heart controul;
Thy eager Transports dwell upon his Soul:
He weighs the well-turn'd *Ball's* experienc'd Force,

---

*The poem celebrates Kent's victory over All-England at the Artillery on 18 June 1744

And guides the rapid *Ball's* impetuous Course,
His supple Limbs with nimble Labour plies,
Nor bends the Grass beneath him as he flies.
The joyous Conquests of the late flown Year,
In Fancy's Paint, with all their Charms appear,
And now again he views the long wish'd Season near,
O thou, sublime Inspirer of my Song!
What matchless Trophies to thy Worth belong!
Look round the Globe, inclin'd to Mirth, and see
What daring Sport can claim the Prize from thee!

   Not puny *Billiards*, where, with sluggish Pace,
The dull *Ball trails* before the feeble *Mace*.
Where no triumphant Shouts, no Clamours dare
Pierce thro' the vaulted Roof and wound the Air;
But stiff Spectators quite inactive stand,
Speechless attending to the *Striker's* Hand:
Where nothing can your languid Spirits move,
Save when the *Marker* bellows out, *Six Love!*
Or when the Ball, *close cushion'd*, slides askew,
And to the op'ning *Pocket runs, a Cou.*

   Nor yet that happier Game, where the smooth Bowl,
In circling Mazes, wanders to the Goal;
Where, much divided between Fear and Glee,
The Youth cries *Rub; O Flee, you Ling'rer, Flee!*

   Not *Tennis* self, thy sister Sport, can charm,
Or with thy fierce Delights our Bosoms warm.
Tho' full of Life, at Ease alone dismay'd,
She calls each swelling Sinew to her Aid;
Her ecchoing Courts confess the sprightly Sound,
While from the *Racket* the brisk Balls rebound.
Yet, to small Space confin'd, ev'n she must yield
To nobler Cricket, the disputed Field.

   O Parent *Britain*! Minion of Renown!
Whose far-extended Fame all Nations own;
Of Sloth-promoting Sports, forewarn'd beware!
Nor think thy Pleasures are thy meanest Care;
Shun with Disdain the squeaky Masquerade,
Where fainting Vice calls Folly to her Aid.
Leave the dissolving Song, the baby Dance,
To soothe the Slaves of *Italy* and *France*:
While the firm Limb, and strong brac'd Nerve are thine.
Scorn Eunuch Sports; to manlier Games incline;
Feed on the Joys that Health and Vigour give;
Where Freedom reigns, 'tis worth the while to live.

Nurs'd on thy Plains, first Cricket learnt to please,
And taught thy Sons to slight inglorious Ease:
And see where busy Counties strive for Fame,
Each greatly potent at this *mighty* Game!
Fierce *Kent*, ambitious of the first Applause,
Against the World combin'd asserts her Cause;
Gay *Sussex* sometimes triumphs o'er the Field,
And fruitful *Surrey* cannot brook to yield.
While *London*, Queen of Cities! proudly vies,
And often grasps the well-disputed Prize.

Thus while *Greece* triumph'd o'er the *barb'rous* Earth,
Seven Cities struggl'd which gave *Homer* birth.

BOOK II

The Argument of the Second Book. – Kent challenges all the other Counties. The Match determined. A Description of the Place of Contest. The particular Qualifications and Excellencies of each Player. The Counties go in.

And now the sons of *Kent* immortal grown,
By a long Series of acquir'd Renown,
Smile at each weak Attempt to shake their Fame;
And thus with vaunting Pride, their Might proclaim.
Long have we bore the Palm, triumphant still,
No County fit to match our wond'rous Skill:
But that all tamely may confess our Sway,
And own us Masters of the glorious Day;
Pick the best Sportsmen from each sev'ral *Shire*,
And let them, if they dare, 'gainst Us appear:
Soon will we prove the Mightiness we boast,
And make them feel their Error, to their Cost.

Fame quickly gave the bold Defiance vent,
And magnify'd th' undaunted sons of *Kent*.
The boastful Challenge sounded far and near;
And spreading, reach'd at length Great *Newland's* Ear:
Where, with his Friend, all negligent he laugh'd,
And threatened future Glories, as they quaff'd.
Struck with the daring Phrase, a piercing Look
On *Bryan* first he cast, and thus he spoke.

And dare the Slaves this paltry Message own!
What then is *Newland's* Arm no better known?
Have I for this the *Ring's* wide Ramparts broke?
Whilst *Romney* shudder'd at the mighty Stroke.
Now by *Alcmena's* sinew'd Son, I swear,
Whose dreadful Blow no mortal Strength can bear!
By *Hermes*, Offspring too of thund'ring *Jove*!
Whose winged Feet like nimble Lightning move!

By ev'ry Patron of the pleasing War,
My chief Delight, my Glory and my Care!
This Arm shall cease the far-driv'n Ball to throw
Shrink from the *Bat* and feebly shun the Blow;
The Trophies, from this conq'ring Forehead torn,
By Boys and Women shall in Scorn be worn
E'er I neglect to let these Blust'rers know,
There live who dare oppose, and beat them too.
Illustrious *Bryan*! Now's the Time to prove
To Cricket's Charms thy much experienc'd Love.
Let us with Care, each hardy Friend inspire!
And fill their Souls with emulating Fire!
Come on . . . True Courage never is dismay'd.
He spoke . . . The Hero listen'd, and obey'd.

   Urg'd by their Chiefs, the Friends of Cricket hear,
And joyous in the fated Lists appear.
The Day approach'd. To view the charming Scene,
Exulting Thousands croud the levell'd Green.

   A place there is, where City-Warriors meet,
Wisely determin'd, not to fight, but eat.
Where harmless Thunder rattles to the Skies,
While the plump *Buff-coat* fires, and shuts his Eyes.
To the pleas'd Mob the bursting Cannons tell
At ev'ry circ'ling Glass, how much they swill.
Here, in the Intervals of Bloodless War,
The Swains with milder Pomp their Arms prepare.
Wide o'er th' extended Plain, the circling String
Restrains th' impatient Throng, and marks a Ring.
But if encroaching on forbidden Ground,
The heedless Croud o'erleaps the proper Bound;
Smith plies, with strenuous Arm, the smacking Whip,
Back to the Line th' affrighted Rebels skip.

   The Stumps are pitch'd. Each Heroe now is seen,
Springs o'er the Frence, and bounds along the Green
In decent White, most gracefully array'd,
Each strong-built Limb in all its Pride display'd.

   Now *Muse*, exert thy Vigour, and describe
The mighty Chieftains of each glorious Tribe!
Bold *Romney* first, before the *Kentish* Band
God-like appear'd, and seiz'd the chief Command.
Judicious Swain! whose quick-discerning Soul
Observes the various Seasons as they roll.
Well-skill'd to spread the thriving Plant around;
And paint with fragrant Flow'rs th' enamell'd Ground.
Conscious of Worth, with Front erect he moves,
And poises in his Hand the *Bat* he loves.

Him *Dorset's* Prince protects, whose youthful Heir
Attends with ardent Glee the mighty Play'r.
He, at *Mid-wicket*, disappoints the Foe;
Springs at the coming Ball and mocks the Blow.
Ev'n thus the *Rattle-snake*, as Trav'lers say,
With stedfast Eye observes it's destin'd Prey;
Till fondly gazing on the glitt'ring Balls,
Into her Mouth th' unhappy Victim falls.
The baffled Hero quits his Bat with Pain,
And mutt'ring lags across the shouting Plain.
Brisk *Hodswell* next strides on with comely Pride,
Tough as the subject of his Trade, the *Hide*.
In his firm Palm, the hard-bound Ball he bears,
And mixes joyous with his pleas'd Compeers.
Bromlean Mills attends the *Kentish* Throng;
And *Robin* from his Size, surnam'd the *Long*.
Six more, as ancient Custom has thought meet,
With willing Steps, th' intrepid Band compleat.
On th' adverse Party, tow'ring o'er the rest,
Left-handed *Newland* fires each arduous Breast.
From many a bounteous Crop, the foodful Grain
With swelling Stores rewards his useful Pain:
While the glad *Farmer*, with delighted Eyes,
Smiles to behold his close-cram'd Gran'rise rise.
Next *Bryan* came, whose cautious Hand could fix
In neat disposed Array the well-pil'd Bricks:
With him, *alone*, scarce any Youth wou'd dare
At single Wicket, try the doubtful War.
For few, save him, th' exalted Honour claim
To play with Judgment, all the various Game.
Next, his accomplish'd Vigour, *Cuddy* tries;
Whose shelt'ring Hand the neat-form'd Garb supplies.
To the dread Plain her *Dane Surrey* sends,
And *Waymark* on the jovial Train attends.
Equal in Numbers, bravely they begin
The dire Dispute. – *The Foes of* Kent *go in.*

BOOK III

The Argument of the Third Book. – The Game. Five on the Side of the Counties are out for three Notches. The Odds run high on the Side of Kent. Bryan and Newland go in; they help the Game greatly. Bryan is unfortunately put out by Kips. Kent, the first Innings, is Thirteen a-head. The Counties go in again, and get Fifty-seven a-head. Kent, in the Second Innings, is very near losing, the two last men being in. Weymark unhappily misses a Catch, and by that means Kent is victorious.

With wary Judgment, scatter'd o'er the Green,
Th' ambitious Chiefs of fruitful *Kent* are seen.
Some, at a Distance, for the *Long Ball* wait,
Some, nearer planted, seize it from the *Bat*.

Hodswell and *Mills* behind the *Wickets* stand,
And each by Turns, the flying Ball command:
Four times from *Hodswell's* Arm it skims the Grass;
Then *Mills* succeeds. The Seekers-out change Place.
Observe, cries *Hodswell*, to the wond'ring Throng,
Be Judges now, whose Arms are better strung!
He said – then pois'd, and rising as he threw,
Swift from his Arm the fatal Missive flew.
Nor with more Force the Death conveying Ball,
Springs from the Cannon to the batter'd Wall;
Nor swifter yet the pointed Arrows go,
Launch'd from the Vigour of the *Parthian* Bow.
It whizz'd along, with unimagin'd Force,
And bore down all, resistless in its Course.
To such impetuous Might compell'd to yield
The *Bail*, and mangled *Stumps* bestrew the Field.

Now glows with ardent Heat th' unequal Fray,
While *Kent* usurps the Honours of the Day;
Loud from the *Ring* resounds the piercing Shout,
Three *Notches* only gain'd, five *Leaders* out.

But while the drooping *Play'r* invokes the Gods,
The busy *Better* calculates his *Odds*,
Swift round the Plain, in buzzing Murmurs run,
I'll hold you Ten to Four, Kent. *– Done Sir. – Done.*

What Numbers can with equal Force, describe
Th' increasing Terrors of the losing Tribe!
When, vainly striving 'gainst the conq'ring Ball,
They see their boasted Chiefs, dejected fall!
Now the two mightiest of the fainting Host
Pant to redeem the Fame their Fellows lost.
Eager for Glory; – For the worst prepared;
With pow'rful Skill, their threat'ned *Wickets* guard.
Bryan, collected for the deadly Stroke,
First cast to *Heav'n* a supplicating Look;
They pray'd. – *Propitious Pow'rs! Assist my Blow,
And grant the flying Orb may shock the Foe!*
This said; he wav'd his *Bat* with forceful Swing,
And drove the batter'd Pellet o'er the Ring.
Then rapid *five times* cross'd the shining Plain,
E'er the departed Ball return'd again.

Nor was thy Prowess valiant *Newland*, mean,
Whose strenuous Arm increas'd the Game *eighteen*;
While from thy Stroke, the Ball retiring hies,
Uninterrupted Clamours rend the Skies.
But oh, what horried Changes oft' are seen,
When faithless Fortune seems the most serene!

Beware, unhappy *Bryan*! oh beware!
Too headless Swain, when such a Foe is near.
Fir'd with Success, elated with his Luck,
He glow'd with Rage, regardless how he struck;
But, forc'd the fatal Negligence to mourn,
Kips crush'd his *Stumps*, before the Youth could turn.
The rest of their unavailing Vigour try,
And by the Pow'r of *Kent*, demolish'd die.
Awakened *Eccho* speaks the *Innings* o'er,
And forty *Notches* deep indent the Score.

   Now *Kent* prepares her better Skill to shew;
Loud rings the Ground, at each tremendous Blow.
With nervous Arm, performing God-like Deeds,
Another, and another Chief succeeds;
'Till, tired with Fame, the conq'ring Host give Way;
And head by *thirteen* Strokes, the toilsome Fray.

   Fresh rous'd to Arms, each Labour-loving Swain
Swells with new Strength, and dares the Field again
Again to *Heav'n* aspires the Chearful Sound;
The *Strokes* re-eccho o'er the spacious Ground.
The *Champion* strikes. When, scarce arriving fair,
The glancing Ball mounts upwards in the Air?
The *Batsman* sees it, and with mournful Eyes,
Fix'd on th' ascending *Pellet* as it flies,
Thus suppliant Claims the Favour of the Skies.
O mighty *Jove*! and all ye Pow'rs above!
Let my regarded Pray'r your pity move!
Grant me but this. Whatever Youth shall dare
Snatch at the Prize, descending thro' the Air;
Lay him extended on the grassy Plain,
And make his bold, ambitious Effort vain.

   He said. The Powers, attending his Request
Granted one Part, to Winds consign'd the rest.

   And now Illustrious *Sackville*, where he stood,
Th' approaching Ball with cautious Pleasure view'd;
At once he sees the Chiefs impending Doom
And pants for mighty Honours, yet to come:
Swift as the *Falcon*, darting on its Prey,
He springs elastick o'er the verdant Way;
Sure of Success, flies upward with a Bound,
Derides the slow Approach, and spurns the Ground.

   The *Counties* now the Game triumphant lead,
And vaunt their Numbers fifty-seven *a Head*.

To end th' immortal Honours of the Day
The *Chiefs of Kent*, once more, their Might essay;
No trifling Toil ev'n yet remains untry'd,
Nor mean the Numbers of the adverse *Side*.
With doubled Skill each dang'rous Ball they shun,
Strike with observing Eye, with Caution run.
At length they know the wish'd for Number near,
Yet wildly pant, and *almost own* they fear.
The two last *Champions* even now are in,
And but three Notches yet remain to win.
When, almost ready to recant it's Boast,
Ambitious *Kent* within an Ace had lost;
The mounting Ball, again obliquely driv'n,
Cuts the pure *Aether*, soaring up to Heav'n.
Waymark was ready: *Waymark*, all must own,
As sure a Swain to catch as e'er was known;
Yet, whether *Jove*, and all-compelling Fate,
In their high Will determin'd *Kent* should beat;
Or the lamented Youth too much rely'd
On sure Success, and *Fortune* often try'd.
The erring Ball, amazing to be told!
Slip'd thro' his out-stretched Hand, and mock'd his Hold.

And now the Sons of *Kent* compleat the Game,
And firmly fix their everlasting Fame.

Anonymous

18th century

Bowling

The rudiments of sciences
    In bowling may be found;
For 'tis in vain to think to bowl,
    'Till you first know the ground.

The fickleness of fortune
    In emblem here is seen;
For often those that touch the block
    Are thrown out of the green.

Of courtiers and of bowlers,
    The fortune is the same;
Each jostles t'other out of place,
    And plays a sep'rate game.

    The jack is like a young coquet;
      Each bowl resembles man;
    They follow wheresoe'er she leads
      As close as e'er they can.

    For tho' in other gaming
      A blockhead be in jest,
    Who gets nearest to the block-head,
      In bowling is the best.

James Grahame

1765–1811

from *British Georgics*

  How rival parishes, and shrievedoms, keep,
On upland lochs, the long expected tryst,
To play their yearly bonspiel. Aged men,
Smit with the eagerness of youth, are there,
While love of conquest lights their beamless eyes,
Now nerves their aims, and makes them young once more.

  The sides when ranged, the distance meted out,
And duly traced the tees, some younger hand
Begins, with throbbing heart, and far o'ershoots,
Or sideward leaves, the mark. In vain he bends
His waist, and winds his hand, as if it still
Retained the power to guide the devious stone;
Which onward hurling, makes the circling group
Quick start aside, to shun its reckless force,
But more and still more skilful aims succeed,
And near and nearer still around the tee,
This side, now that, approaches, till at last,
Two seem equidistant, straws or twigs
Decide as umpires 'tween contending coits.

  Then, keener still, as life itself were staked,
Kindles the friendly strife; one points the like
To him who, poising, aims and aims again.
Another runs and sweeps where nothing lies.
Success, alternately from side to side,

Changes, and quick the hours unnoted fly
Till light begins to fail, and, deep below,
The player, as he stoops to lift his coit,
Sees, half incredulous, the rising moon.

And now the final, the decisive spiel
Begins; near and more near the sounding stones
Come winding in, some bearing straight along,
Crowd jostling all around the mark; while one
Just slightly touching, victory depends
Upon the final aim. Long swings the stone,
Then with full force, careering furious on,
Rattling, it strikes aside both friend and foe,
Maintains its course, and takes the victor's place.
The social meal succeeds, and social glass;
In words the fight renewed is fought again,
While festive mirth forgets the winged hours.

James Hogg
1770–1835

The Channel Stane

Air – 'Highland Harry'

Of a' the games that e'er I saw,
   Man, callant, laddie, birkie, wean,
The dearest, far aboon them a',
   Was aye the witching channel stane.
        Chorus
      Oh! for the channel-stane!
        The fell good name the channel-stane!
      There's no a game that e'er I saw,
        Can match auld Scotland's channel-stane.

I've been at bridals unco glad,
   Wi' courting lasses woundrous fain,
But what is a' the fun I've had,
   Compare it wi' the channel stane?
     Oh! for, &c.

I've played at quoiting in my day,
   And may be I may do't again,
But still unto myself I'd say,
   This is no the channel-stane.
     Oh! for, &c.

Were I a sprite in younder sky,
  Never to come back again,
I'd sweep the moon and starlets by,
  And beat them at the channel-stane.
    Oh! for, &c.

We'd boom across the milky way,
  One tee should be the Northern Wain,
Another, bright Orion's ray,
  A comet for a channel-stane.
    Oh! for, &c.

Anonymous

1782

The Tennis-Court

When as the hand at Tennis plays,
  And Men to gaming fall;
Love is the court, Hope is the house,
  And favour serves the Ball.

This Ball itself is due desert,
  The Line that measure shows
Is Reason, whereon judgement looks
  Where Players win and lose.

The Tutties are deceitful shifts;
  The Stoppers, jealousy,
Which hath, Sire Argus' hundred eyes,
  Wherewith to watch and pry.

The Fault, whereon fifteen is lost,
  Is want of Wit and Sense;
And he that brings the Racket in
  Is Double Diligence.

But now the Racket is Free-will,
  Which makes the Ball rebound;
And noble beauty is the choice,
  And of each Game the ground.

The Racket strikes the Ball away,
  And there is oversight;
A bandy, ho! the people cry,
  And so the Ball takes flight.

Now at the length good liking proves
    Content to be their gain;
Thus, in the Tennis-Court, Love is
    A Pleasure mixed with Pain.

Anonymous
1792

'To box, or not to box' *

To box, or not to box, that is the question,
Whether it is nobler in the mind to suffer
The stings and goadings of a well-tweak'd nose,
Or to take heart with Humphries or Mendoza,
And by opposing end them. To strip, to bear
No more; and by this movement then to say we end
The heart-ache and a thousand natural jeers
The coward's heir to. 'Tis a consummation
Devoutly to be wish'd. To strip, to square,
To fight – perchance to beat. Aye, there's the rub,
For in that daring step, what blows may come.
When we have shuffled off our coats and shirts
Must give us pause; there's the respect
That makes this diffidence of so long life.
For who would bear the taunts and sneers o' the mob;
The pangs of cold neglect and fame's delay
The porter's wrongs – the coal-heaver's contumely,
Th' insolence of pugilists, and the spurns
That patient merit of the hero takes,
When he himself might his quietus make
With a well-put blow. Who would insults bear,
And fret and fume beneath a doubtful state.
But that a dread of something in the stage,
The undetermin'd trial, from whose bourn,
Earle ne'er return'd, puzzles the will,
And makes us rather bear those ills we have,
Than fly to others than we know not of.
Thus fear of drubbing makes us cowards all,
And thus the wish of native resolution,
And skill'd manœuvres of each well-grac'd ring,
With this regard, their profits turn away,
And lose the fame of boxing.

---

*Earle died after sustaining a blow to the head in his fight with Tom Tyne, 'The Tailor', before the Prince of Wales at Brighton racecourse on 6 August 1788.

William Wordsworth

1770–1850

from *The Prelude*

And in the frosty season, when the sun
Was set, and visible for many a mile
The cottage windows blazed through twilight gloom,
I heeded not their summons: happy time
It was indeed for all of us – for me
It was a time of rapture! Clear and loud
The village clock tolled six, – I wheeled about,
Proud and exulting like an untired horse
That cares not for his home. All shod with steel,
We hissed along the polished ice in games
Confederate, imitative of the chase
And woodland pleasures, – the resounding horn,
The pack loud chiming, and the hunted hare.
So through the darkness and the cold we flew,
And not a voice was idle; with the din
Smitten, the precipices rang aloud;
The leafless trees and every icy crag
Tinkled like iron; while far distant hills
Into the tumult sent an alien sound
Of melancholy not unnoticed, while the stars
Eastward were sparkling clear, and in the west
The orange sky of evening died away.

Samuel Taylor Coleridge

1772–1834

Lines composed while climbing the left ascent of Brockley Coomb, in the County of Somerset, May, 1795

With many a pause and oft reverted eye
I climb the Coomb's ascent: sweet songsters near
Warble in shade their wild-wood melody:
Far off th' unvarying Cuckoo soothes my ear.
Up soar the startling stragglers of the Flock
That on green plots o'er precipices brouze:
From the forc'd fissures of the naked rock
The Yew tree bursts! Beneath its dark green boughs
(Mid which the May-thorn blends its blossoms white)
Where broad smooth stones jut out in mossy seats,

I rest. – And now have gain'd the topmost site.
Ah! What a luxury of landscape meets
My gaze! Proud Towers, and Cots more dear to me,
Elm-shadow'd Fields, and prospect-bounding Sea!
Deep sighs my lonely heart; I drop the tear:
Enchanting spot! O were my SARA here!

Frederick Lawson

19th century

*Chaunt for Tom Cribb**

Come, listen, all ye fighting gills
And coves of boxing note, sirs,
Whilst I relate some bloody mills,
   In our time have been fought, sirs,
Whoe'er saw Ben and Tom display,
   Could tell a pretty story,
The milling-bout they got that day,
   Send both ding-dong to glory.
           Singing fal la la, etc.

Now Ben he left it in his will
   As all his pals declare it,
That who the hero's chair would fill
   Must win it or not wear it;
No tainted miller he could stand,
   Right sound must be his cat's-meat,
Who could not bear his hide well tanned,
   Was quite unfit for that seat.

All nations came to claim the prize,
   Amongst them many a don, sirs,
And Bill Ward swore, b—t his eyes,
   He'd mill 'em every one, sirs,
At Bexley Heath, it hapt one day,
   He was beaten black and blue, sirs,
By one deep in the Fancy lay,
   'Twas little Dan, the Jew, sirs.

*This chaunt, sung at a dinner in honour of Tom Cribb, begins by reminding the listener that 'Big Ben' Brain became undisputed Champion of England by defeating Tom Johnson in eighteen rounds on 17 January 1791; it also makes reference to Bill Warr, Daniel Mendoza, Young 'the Ruffian', Isaac Bittoon, Samuel 'Dutch Sam' Elias, Tom Belcher, Henry 'The Game Chicken' Pearce, Jack Gully. Captain Barclay, cited after the catalogue of pugilists, was Cribb's patron.

The Ruffian, Young, next on the list,
  Laid claim to boxing merits,
A mere pretender to the fist,
  Who dwelt in wine and spirits.
His hits were RUM none could deny,
  His blackstrap none could bear it,
But of his hogshead he was shy,
  Lest they should tap his claret.

BITTON then came, a champion bold,
  And dealt some hard and sly knocks,
But yet when all the truth is told
  Some rank him with the shy cocks;
But prate like this we must not mind,
  A Dutchman true begot him,
Whoe'er has seen BITTON behind,
  Will ne'er dispute his bottom.

Of all the milling coves the crack,
  None pleases more than Sam, sirs,
Whose whiskers are of jetty black,
  As those of whip, Jeram, sirs,
So neatly fibs the Israelite,
  To every stander-by, sirs,
Who must allow it has a sight,
  Worth well a Jew's eye, sirs.

We now must sing of Belcher's fame,
  Whose race was full of glory;
His matchless deeds I need not name,
  You all must know his story.
He beat the best coves of his day,
  But few could stand before him,
For he could hit and get away,
  If not – why he could floor them.

Champion of the milling corps,
  Next starts a true Game Chicken,
His honours to the last he bore,
  But never bore a licking;
Till tyrant Death, man's greatest foe,
  Who mercy shows him never,
Hit poor Pearce a mortal blow,
  Which closed his eyes for ever.

Jack Gully made a manly stand
  In science quite complete, sirs,
He rather chose to fight on land,
  Than serve longer in the fleet, sirs.
Where many worthies of their line,

Like Jack for bravery noted,
  Are under hatches left to pine,
    Nor hopes to be promoted.

Next rings the fame of gallant Cribb,
  A cool and steady miller,
Who late in Yorkshire went to fib
  A first-rate man of colour.
No matter whether black or white,
  No tint of skin could save him,
A horse's kick was pure delight,
  To the belly punch he gave him.

England's champion now behold,
  In him who fills the chair, sirs,
Who never yet a battle sold,
  Nor lost one in despair, sirs,
For in each contest or set-to,
  Brave Tom bore off the laurel,
Which proudly planted on his brow,
  Says – 'Touch me at your peril.'

Now fill your glasses to the brim,
  And honour well my toast, sirs,
'May we be found in fighting trim,
  When Boney treads our coasts, sirs.'
The gallant Barclay shall lead on,
  The Fancy lads adore him,
And Devil or Napoleon,
  Leave us alone to floor him.

Bob Gregson

1778–1824

*British Lads and Black Millers**

'You gentlemen of fortune, attend unto my ditty,
  A few lines I have penn'd upon this great fight,
In the centre of England the noble place is pitch'd on,
  For the valour of this country, or America's delight;
    The sturdy Black doth swear,
    The moment he gets there,

*See footnote on p.28

The planks the stage is built on, he'll make them blaze and smoke,
    Then Cribb with smiling face,
    Says these boards I'll ne'er disgrace,
They're relations of mine; they're old English oak.

'Brave Molineaux replied, I've never been denied,
  To fight the foes of Briton on such planks as those,
If relationship you claim, by and by you'll know my name,
  I'm the Moorish milling blade that can drub my foes.
    The Cribb replied with haste,
    You slave I will you baste,
As your master us'd to cane you, t'will bring thing to your mind.
    If from bondage you've got clear,
    To impose on Britons here,
You'd better stop with Christopher, you'll quickly find.

'The garden of freedom is the British land we live in,
  And welcomes every slave from his banished land,
Allows them to impose on a nation good and generous,
  To incumber and pollute our native soil.
    But John Bull cries out loud,
    We're neither poor nor proud,
But open to all nations, let them come from where they will.
    The British lads that's here,
    Quite strangers are to fear,
Here's Tom Cribb, with bumper round, for he can them mill.'

Thomas Moore

1779–1852

*Epistle from Tom Cribb to Big Ben**

Concerning Some Foul Play in a Late Transaction

'Ahi, mio BEN!' – METASTASIO.'

WHAT! BEN, my old hero, is this your renown?
  Is *this* the new *go*? – kick a man when he's down!
When the foe has knock'd under, to tread on him then –
  By the fist of my father, I blush for thee, BEN!

'Foul! foul!' all the lads of the Fancy exclaim –
CHARLEY SHOCK is electrified – BELCHER spits flame –
And MOLYNEUX – ay, even BLACKY cries 'shame!'
Time was when JOHN BULL little difference spied
'Twixt the foe at his feet, and the friend at his side:
When he found (such his humour in fighting and eating)
His foe, like his beef-steak, the sweeter for beating.
But this comes, Master BEN, of your curst foreign notions,
Your trinkets, wigs, thingumbobs, gold lace and lotions;
Your Noyeaus, Curaçoas, and the Devil knows what –
(One swig of *Blue Ruin* is worth the whole lot!)
Your great and small *crosses* – (my eyes, what a brood!
A *cross*-buttock from *me* would do some of them good!)
Which have spoilt you, till hardly a drop, my old porpoise,
Of pure English *claret* is left in your *corpus*;
And (as JIM says) the only one trick, good or bad,
Of the Fancy you're up to, is *fibbing*, my lad.
Hence it comes, – BOXIANA, disgrace to thy page! –
Having floor'd, by good luck, the first *swell* of the age,
Having conquer'd the *prime one*, that *mill'd* us all round,
You kick'd him, old BEN, as he gasp'd on the ground!
Ay – just at the time to show spunk, if you'd got any –
Kick'd him, and jaw'd him, and *lag'd* him to Botany.
Oh, shade of the *Cheesemonger!* you, who, alas,
Doubled up, by the dozen, those Mounseers in brass,
On that great day of *milling*, when blood lay in lakes,
When Kings held the bottle, and Europe the stakes,
Look down upon BEN – see him, *dunghill* all o'er.
Insult the fall'n foe, that can harm him no more!
Out, cowardly *spooney!* – again and again,
By the fist of my father, I blush for thee, BEN.
To *show the white feather* is many men's doom,
But, what of *one* feather? – BEN shows a *whole Plume*.

*'Big Ben' was originally Benjamin Brain, Champion of England from 1786 to 1791, and the nickname was given to the Prince Regent; the 'late transaction' was Napoleon's transportation to St Helena; the 'Cheesemonger' refers to John Shaw, 'The Life Guardsman', a pugilist who was killed at Waterloo.

Anonymous

19th century

Crib and the Black*

On the eighteenth of December of a fight I will sing,
When bold Crib and Molineux entered the ring,
With hope and expectation our bosoms beating high,
While the rain pour'd in torrents from a dark low'ring sky.
                                          Chorus – With hope, &c.

Tom Crib is a British man, he's cast in British mould,
With a heart like a lion, of courage stout and bold.
A brave black man is Molineux, from America he came,
And boldly tried to enter with Crib the lists of fame.

The Black stripp'd, and appeared of a giant-like strength,
Large in bone, large in muscle, and with arms a cruel length,
With his skin as black as ebony – Crib as white as snow,
They shook hands like good fellows, then to it they did go.

The very first round they had Crib hit him on the head,
But receiv'd one in the mouth, and very freely he bled,
The two or three next rounds Crib seem'd to have the best,
But the Black man most bravely resolved to stand the test.

Then the Black he did rally, Oh, how he play'd away,
And shew'd our British hero some terrible hard play,
Like light'ning 'bout Crib's *napper* the blows came left and right,
While the Black's friends felt certain their man would win the fight.

Then the Black still bore on with a terrible great force,
The blows fell on poor Tom Crib like kicks from a horse.
His friends e'en were doubtful, Crib will lose it they did cry,
Never mind, says he to Gully, *I'd be better bye and bye.*

Look! how cautious he fights now, how his distance he does mind,
He's coming about, my boys, see he's got his second wind,
He's sure to bring us thro' my boys, spite of all the Black's power,
Hark! he's *come it* to old Joey Ward, he can fight a good hour.

---

*The first fight between Tom Cribb, Champion of England, and Tom Molineux, 'The Black', was one of the most dramatic encounters in boxing history. It took place at Copthall Common, East Grinstead, on 18 December 1810 and Molineux might have won in the twenty-eighth round had not Cribb's second Joe Ward played for time so his man could recover; eventually the fight was stopped after fifty-five minutes in the thirty-third round when Molineux admitted 'I can fight no more'.

For many a hard round each the prize did strive to gain,
They had fought fifty minutes in the cold shiv'ring rain,
Belcher saw them down together, to Bill Gibbons he did say,
I'm down upon Crib's mug, Bill, he's sure to win the day.

Now Crib seem'd to get better and stronger every round,
And four times he fairly brought the Black to the ground,
The Black's strength forsook him, he'd not a chance to win.
He fought like a brave fellow, but was forc'd to give in.

Ye swells, ye flash, ye milling coves, who this hard fight see,
Let us drink to these heroes, come join along with me,
A bumper to brave Crib, boys, to the Black a bumper too,
Tho' beat, he prov'd a man my boys, what more could a man do.

Tom Hazel

19th century

*Multum in Parvo, or a Miracle in Twenty Minutes**

A true Briton from Bristol, a rum one to fibb,
He's champion of England, his name is TOM CRIB,
With white and black men, has mill'd all round,
But one to mill him in the world can't be found.

No curs he ever fought, but good men they all were,
Which proves him a good one, all must now declare,
For of strength he has much, and of science no lack,
And of bottom a plenty he found for the Black.

The Black's a good man we know very well,
But CRIB is a better, and the same you can tell,
For his pluck is so lasting, and his courage so bold,
That he, Champion like, has again won their gold.

For Six Hundred they fought, no paltry sum,
Which by many was said, by the Black would be won;
But without prejudice to colour, and see it thousands did,
Molineaux, 'gainst his will, by our Champion was fibb'd.

---

*Tom Cribb's second championship fight with Tom Molineux, 'The Black', on 28 September 1811, ended after nineteen minutes ten seconds when the challenger was unable to stand in the eleventh round.

Fair play to the parties was shewn, you'll admit,
Though Blackee was strong, with CRIB could not hit,
And of his milling the Black has had slice upon slice,
Though giants in stature, in his hands are but mice.

Oft enough they have tried to convince 'em its a joke,
To value the shadow of fir with the substance of oak,
Which its virtue retains for ages we are sure,
And high in perfection, when firs are no more.

Anonymous

19th century

'Pray, havn't you heard'

Pray, havn't you heard of a jolly young coal-heaver,*
   Who down at Hungerford us'd for to ply,
His daddles he us'd with such skill and dexterity,
   Winning each mill, sirs, and blacking each eye.
   He sparred so neat, and fought so steadily,
   He hit so straight, and he won so readily;
And now he's a coal-merchant, why should he care,
Tho' his dealings are black yet his actions are fair.

To mention the times that he's won by hard milling,
   'Tis useless to tell unto anyone here,
For tho' no Adonis, he's very nigh killing,
   His arguments have such an effect on the ear.
   He hit half rounds, and he fought so steadily,
   He mill'd away and he won so readily.
Then why should this coal-merchant ever know care,
Tho' his dealings are black yet his actions are fair.

A cove in the black line, he show'd opposition,
   So Tommy determined to give him a turn;
And Molineaux made him a bold proposition,
   But twice he has found that his coals wouldn't burn.
   For he sparred so neat and fought so steadily,
   He hit so straight and he won so readily;
For why should this coal-merchant ever know care,
While he's champion of England, and now fills the chair.

---

*Before setting up as a publican in London, Tom Cribb attempted unsuccessfully to operate as a coal-merchant at Hungerford Wharf.

Anonymous
19th century

A-Boxing we will go

Come, move the song and stir the glass,
    For why should we be sad;
Let's drink to some free-hearted lass,
    And Cribb, the boxing lad.
        And a-boxing we will go, will go, will go,
        And a-boxing we will go.

Italians stab their friends, behind,
    In darkest shades of night,
But Britons they are bold and kind,
    And box their friends by light.

The sons of France their pistols use,
    Pop, pop, and they have done,
But Britons with the hands will bruise,
    And scorn away to run.

Throw pistols, poinards, swords aside,
    And all such deadly tools,
Let boxing be the Briton's pride,
    The science of their schools.

Since boxing is a manly game,
    And Britons' recreation,
By boxing we will raise our fame,
    'Bove any other nation.

If Boney doubt it let him come,
    And try with Cribb a round,
And Cribb shall beat him like a drum,
    And make his carcass sound.

Mendoza, Gully, Molineaux,
    Each nature's weapon wield,
Who each at Boney would stand true,
    And never him to yield.

We've many more would like to floor
    The little upstart king,
And soon for mercy make him roar,
    Within a spacious ring.

A fig for Boney – let's have done,
   With that ungracious name,
We'll drink and pass our days in fun,
   And box to raise our fame.
         And a-boxing, etc.

Anonymous

19th century

*Monody on the Death of Dick Curtis**

Farewell! a long farewell! renowned King Dick!
Well may we mourn that thou has cut thy stick;
Victorious still in many a sharp attack,
Stern Champion, Death, hath laid thee on thy back;
Exhausted all thy bottom and thy pluck,
Thine arm lies powerless, and thy colours struck;
Rigid thine elasticity of limb,
Deaf are thy listeners, and thy ogles dim;
Pale are those lips from which rich humour rush'd,
Spun are thy spicy yarns, thy tongue is hush'd;
Stripped are the laurels bright that girt thy brow
And dust to dust is all that waits thee now.

Yet long the Fancy's tears thy grave shall wet,
Star of the Light Weights, all-accomplished Pet!
For thy bold spirit soared on eagle's wing,
And shed a halo round the fighting Ring –
Acknowledged there the bravest and the best,
For craven fear ne'er harboured in thy breast;
Conquest, proud conquest, was thine only aim,
Unrivall'd still in gallantry and game.
As lightning quick to dart upon thy foe,
And in the dust to lay his glories low,
The palm of victory forcing him to yield,
And sing 'Peccavi' on the battle-field;
Adieu, thou pride and wonder of the age,
The brightest star on Fistiana's page,
Where records of your manly deeds are stor'd,
The pinks you've pepper'd, and the trumps you've floored!

*Dick Curtis (1802–43), 'The Pet', was Champion of the Light Weights from 1820 to 1828 and celebrated for his skill and speed; his only defeat was at the hands of Jack Perkins, 'The Oxford Pet', in 1828.

Why should we mourn of Perkins the sad tale,
O'er which sad memory fain would draw a veil,
And while unfading thy brave deeds shall bloom,
Consign thine errors with thee to the tomb!

Well may we weep for these degenerate days,
As a sad trophy to thy fame we raise,
And mourn, since boxing hath become a trade,
Its honour tarnished and its flowers decay'd!
No hardy Cribb now throws the gauntlet down,
Nor brave Tom Spring, of unalloyed renown;
No brawny Belcher now for victory strives,
Nor tough Game Chicken flourishes his fives;
No Molyneux now rears his sable nob,
Nor rough-and-ready stout Whiteheaded Bob.
Well may we grieve, as we thy fate deplore,
The golden days of milling are no more,
Exclaiming, as fresh candidates appear,
'Oh, what a woeful falling-off is here!'

But Curtis prov'd a trump, and no mistake,
To every move upon the board awake,
And staunch as e'er tied colours to a stake!
When a mere boy, by two good men assail'd,
Beneath his prowess Brown and Watson quail'd;
And after combat resolute and tough,
Lenney and Cooper, sorrowing, cried, 'Enough!'
Thrice Peter Warren tried to do the trick,
In a turn-up, from momentary heat,
Ned Savage was made savage by defeat;
And bouncing Barney Aaron, Hebrew stout,
Look'd all abroad when Richard sarv'd him out;
Tisdale our Monarch ventur'd to attack,
But all the shine was taken out of Jack;
And lastly Dick, urg'd on by insult's goad,
Whack'd a coalheaver in the Surrey Road.

But his last fight is fought, and clos'd his reign,
And time is call'd to poor King Dick in vain;
For Death, that ruthless monarch, gaunt and grim,
Hath cruelly hit out and finished him,
Sent him to earth, and stiffened every limb.
Flower of the Fancy, yet one more adieu!
Where shall we look to find a 'Pet' like you?
Sound be thy sleep, receive my last good night,
And may the turf upon thy breast be light,
For though in manhood's prime by fate unshipp'd,
Thou wert a boy as brave as ever stripp'd;
Time shall fly forward, years shall wax and wane,
Ere 'we shall look upon thy like again.'

Anonymous

19th century

*Heroic Stanzas from Bendigo to Deaf Burke**

Why, truly, my nabs of the torpid auricular,
Your conduct of late ha'nt been very particular,
And I tell you in verse, which I'm no hand at tagging,
That I shrewdly suspect you of bounding and bragging.

When a challenge you gave, and defiance was hurl'd
To any professor of fives in the world,
Of course I consider'd that nothing was wrong,
Tho' I fancied you com'd it a trifle too strong.

I knew you were brave, and as strong as a horse,
And remembered your sending poor Simon to dorse;
And you told us how Yankees all quak'd at your name,
And 'guessed' they ne'er witness'd such bottom and game.

You swore, as Jem Ward had retir'd on the shelf,
Your mind was made up to be Champion yourself;
And you dar'd all the world to contend for the prize,
While you barred neither country, nor colour, nor size.

This was all wastly well, but how came you to trot
Ere you knew if your challenge was answer'd or not,
And to cut from your quarters in London adrift
On the coming consarn between Adams and Swift?

I tell you, my Deaf 'un, without any flourish,
Your conduct appears most confoundedly currish;
And as straightforward dealing was always my plan,
If you wish for a customer, I am your man.

You boast, my 'Venetian', whoe'er may attack you,
You have lordlings and dukes in attendance to back you;
Well, as folks can't suppose you are telling us fibs,
Pray, are these patricians to fork out the dibs?

I give you my word, Peter Crawley, my crony,
On my part is ready for posting the pony;
How is it, on yours, that your pal, Jemmy Burn,
In spite of your chaffing, keeps dropping astern?

---

*William 'Bendigo' Thomson (1811–80) was Champion of England from 1835 to 1850; when he fought James Burke (1809–45), 'The Deaf 'Un', on 12 February 1839, the Champion outclassed the challenger who was eventually disqualified for butting.

Do you fancy that conduct like this will content us?
Oh, let no folks say of you *'Non est Inwentus;'*
Come forward, if e'er as a man you have felt,
For Bendigo dares you to strive for the belt.

Presume not brave fellows henceforward to taunt,
For though of my prowess I've no wish to vaunt,
An out-and-out good one I fac'd in big Caunt,
Who in stature and muscle match'd owld John of Gaunt.

In capital style you exhibit, I'm told,
As statues of worthies wot figur'd of old;
Apollor, and Wenus, and Mars to the letter –
Wouldn't *Back-us*, my cove, suit a precious deal better?

But perhaps, arter all – such, believe me, my trust is –
I may not exactly be doing you justice;
And when you're aware I will meet you at milling,
At the scratch you may show yourself ready and willing.

It will give me much pleasure, my Deaf'un, I swear,
To see how you'll show off your attitudes there –
While I, glad to see you returned from your mizzling,
As you're partial to statues, may give you a chiselling.

I trust that in Paris you show'd in prime feather,
And that you and old Soult had a bottle together;
I'd like to have seen how you sported your tanners,
And mark the French polish you got on your manners.

But perhaps it is time to leave off, my prime feller,
For I an't wery much of a writer or speller;
Yourself and your pals of the Fancy arn't green,
And will doubtless diskiver at once what I mean.

They may call me a fool, and the words won't affront,
For 'tis sartain they can't say the same of my blunt;
They may swear you are sartain to vanquish me – good –
But pray do not crow till you're out of the wood.

For the present farewell! May we soon have a shy,
And if I don't floor you, my Deaf'un, I'll try –
So off, without any desire to offend, I go,
Remaining, in hopes the best man may win –
                                        'Bendigo'

Anonymous
19th century

The Unfinished Fight of the American Giant and the Tipton Slasher*

Freeman, of giant frame! to thee a welcome warm we gave,
When wafted to the British shores across the Atlantic wave;
In harmony we saw thee move with gallant champion Caunt,
As muscular as Hercules, and tall as John of Gaunt.

We hail'd thee of thy countrymen the model and the flower,
And modest was thy bearing, though possessed of giant power;
Against thee Slander never dar'd her poisoned tongue to wag,
And never was it thine to bounce, to bluster, or to brag.

You came not to our land the gauntlet down to fling,
Here to no conquest you aspired within our battle ring,
But ready to come forward still at Friendship's special call,
To take a fragrant pipe of weed and a cordial cup withal.

'But yet I love my native land, and scorn each action base,
And never *Craven* act of mine a *Freeman* shall disgrace;
Whoever dares me to the fight, by no proud threat'ning scar'd,
Will find me anxious still for peace, and yet for war prepared!'

'By Heavens!' cried Johnny Broome, 'my pink, tho' nothing you're afraid of,
I have a Novice in the Ring who'll try what stuff you're made of,
Deposits shall be duly made, and matters go on snugly,
And there you'll meet a customer as rum as he is ugly.

'One who professes bull-dog game I to the scratch will bring,
Welcome to whom is punishment as flowers in early spring;
One who in contest fierce and long, "Enough!" has never cried,
But rushes forward to his man, and will not be denied.

'The same to him is Briton bold and Transatlantic foeman,
With courage at the sticking-place like ancient Greek or Roman;
Regardless still of body hits, or on the snout a smasher,
BILL PERRY is the trump I mean, the slaughtering Tipton Slasher!'

---

*On 6 December 1842 William Perry, 'The Tipton Slasher', fought Charles Freeman, a seven-foot American, over seventy rounds lasting eighty-four minutes. The fight was abandoned when a fog reduced visibility to a few feet. Although Ben Caunt, the Champion, had brought Freeman to England as an exhibit rather than a boxer he is reckoned to have shared the honours with Perry.

'Bravo! bold Johnny,' Freeman cried, 'then to your text be steady,
Fixed be the time, as well as place, and Freeman's tin is ready;
Into condition get your friend as early as you can,
And trust me I will do my best to floor your Tipton man.'

The heroes trained as fine as stars, with gallantry untam'd,
And in December's dreary month the day of fight was nam'd;
'Who heeds,' the Slasher cried, 'dark days, cold blast, or storm?
We'll have sufficient work cut out to keep our systems warm.

'Tho' twixt the Giant and myself the difference is great,
I care not for his stature high, I care not for his weight,
Nor for his wondrous length of reach does Perry care a whit;
And where so huge a carcass shows, the easier 'tis to hit.'

Thus to Big Caunt the Giant cried, 'My friend, 'tis time to trot,
But bear me witness ere we start, this fight I courted not;
My manly foe, I do not doubt, possesses thorough game,
But if he falls 'tis he alone and Johnny Broome to blame.

'Tho' with your gallant countrymen peace was my only aim,
Boston, New York, and Washington my prowess can proclaim,
And never in my proud career white feather did I show;
Nor ever cut a friend in need, nor shrunk before a foe.'

December sixth in darkness broke, the dawn was chill and damp,
And numerous Fancy toddlers betimes were on the tramp;
Corinthian swells and commoners made simultaneous rush
To Sawbridgeworth, in Hertfordshire, through muck, and mire, and slush.

But how the beaks in wrath proclaim'd, amid the motley race,
That no prize fight or milling match should then and there take place;
And how the pugilists themselves looked very down and blank,
While the spectators made a move both retrograde and flank –

And how they managed after all to give the traps the slip,
And hastening back to Sawbridgeworth prepared at once to strip;
How seventy gallant rounds were fought 'till deepening shades of night,
With its extinguisher forbade the finish of the fight –

And how the assembled multitude with sundry rueful shrugs,
Homeward retraced their weary way with disappointed mugs;
And how in Despond's dismal slough a lot of worthies fell –
Next week the bard of 'London Life' will accurately tell.

But tho' no victory was achieved by well intended thumps,
Both men have proved undoubted game, and turn'd out genuine trumps;
And all uninjur'd and unscath'd in Tuesday's battle fray,
Slasher and Freeman both survive to fight another day.

Anonymous

19th century

Valentine from Bendigo to Brassey*

Many happy returns of the Spring, bouncing Brassey,
    I hope Fortune gives you no cause to complain,
That you're right as a rivet, determined and saucy,
    And ready for mischief with Bendy again.

May I never again take a sip of blue ruin
    If I live to see fair English fighting take wing;
'Tis time for the big 'uns to up and be doing,
    For bantam cocks only show now in the ring.

Then again for the laurel crown let us be tugging,
    May fair play be always our motto and plan;
But Gaunt I denounce and his system of hugging,
    A practice more fit for a bear than a man.

As to Freeman, the giant – I don't mean offending –
    His bulk and his weight may astonish the raw,
But when with Bill Perry, the Slasher, contending
    I'm bless'd if he showed any point worth a straw.

Of falsehood I scorn the unclean manufacture,
    My luck with good men always forward to try;
And but for my knee-pan's unfortunate fracture,
    With the Yankee I wouldn't have shrunk from a shy.

Then, Brassey, come out if you truly mean milling,
    And drip down your dust for a match if you dare,
And you'll find Billy Bendigo ready and willing,
    To give you a sample of Nottingham ware.

I'm anxious, bold Brassey, again to be busy,
    And face a good fellow, true-hearted and tough;
And I'd cheerfully draw from my cly my last tizzy
    To see two game pugilists stripp'd to the buff.

But here I conclude, for my time's up for starting,
    And conscience is giving a sort of shove;
But I just drop a hint, my good fellow, at parting –
    I you can't raise the needful, I'll fight you for love.

---

*On 23 March 1840 Bendigo seriously injured his knee-cap and had to give up boxing. By 1844 he was again ready for action and this broadside represents a challenge to John Leechman, 'Brassey of Bradford'; Brassey, who had been defeated by Bendigo in 1836, could not make a deposit.

Anonymous

19th century

*An Heroic Epistle from Brassey to Big Caunt**

To thee I send these lines, illustrious Caunt,
Of courage tried, and huge as John of Gaunt,
To thee my foolscap with black ink I blot,
To tell the big 'un Brassey fears him not
And that in battle, should the fates allow,
He means to snatch the laurels from his brow,
At all his boasted pluck and prowess smile,
And give him pepper in superior style.

Yes, gallant Caunt, next Tuesday will declare
If you or I the champion's belt shall wear,
And be assured regardless of the tin,
I'll go to work and do my best to win,
Prove that in fight one Briton can surpass ye,
And if you ask his name, I thunder – Brassey.

What proof of milling prowess did you show
In your two scrambling fights with Bendigo?
When of your foeman's punishment aware,
You roughly squeezed him like a polar bear,
Nearly extinguished in his lungs the breath,
And almost hugged him in your arms to death –
Such a base system I pronounce humbugging,
Don't call it fighting, Caunt, I call it hugging,
And if bold Brassey with that game you tease,
The bear may soon be minus of his grease
And for a practice cowardly as foul,
Receive a lesson that may make him growl,
But bounce I bar – plain dealing is my plan,
And in the ring I'll meet you man to man,
And do most certainly the best I can.

May no base beak, or trap with aspect rude,
Upon a comfortable mill intrude –
A mill between not enemies, but friends,
And upon which a lot of blunt depends;
A mill, I trust, which, as in days of yore,
Will honest fighting to the ring restore;

---

*On 26 October 1845 Benjamin Caunt, Champion of England from 1835 to 1845, defeated John Leechman, 'Brassey of Bradford', over one hundred and one rounds in a fight lasting ninety minutes.

A mill which, whosoever may win the same,
Will show the British boxer's genuine game,
Unkind aspersions on the Fancy crush,
And put accurs'd knife-practice to the blush –
In practice which, with bold and fearless face,
In bloody letters stamps our land's disgrace.

But let that pass, while we like boxers bold,
Shall manly contest in the ring uphold,
And settle matters, not with slaughtering knives,
But well-braced muscles and a bunch of fives.
What tho' in battle with some Fancy lad,
An ogle should in mourning suit be clad,
What tho' profusion of straightforward knocks
Should for a while confuse the knowledge box?
Why, these are trifles which a cur may scare,
But teach good men hard punishment to bear,
And as they pass this earthly region through,
All men will have a clumsy thump or two,
And there's no doubt will lessen their complaining,
To meet hard knocks to get them into training;
But Time, my worthy, warns me to desist,
So for a while farewell, my man of fist;
Of your conceit on Tuesday I will strip ye –
On Tuesday next 'I meet you at Philippi':
Till then believe me resolute and saucy,
A foe without one hostile feeling.

        'Brassey'

Anonymous

19th century

*The Combat of Sayerius and Heenanus**

A Lay of Ancient London (supposed to be recounted to his
Great-grandchildren, 17 April 1920, by an Ancient Gladiator)

  Close round my chair, my children,
   And gather at my knee,
  The while your mother poureth
   The Old Tom in my tea;

---

*This parody of Macaulay appeared in *Punch*, 28 April 1860, and was widely thought to be the work of Thackeray. It celebrates the contest between Tom Sayers, Champion of England from 1849 to 1860, and the American John Hennan ('The Benicia Boy') on 17 April 1860.

What while your father quaffeth
   His meagre Bordeaux wine –
'Twas not on such potations
   Were reared these thews o' mine.
Such drinks came in the very year –
   Methinks I mind it well –
That the great fight of HEENANUS
   With SAYERIUS befell.*

These knuckles then were iron,
   This biceps like a cord,
This fist shot from the shoulder
   A bullock would have floored.
CRAWLEIUS his Novice,
   They used to call me then
In the Domus Savilliana†
   Among the sporting men.
There, on benefit occasions,
   The gloves I oft put on,
Walking round to show my muscle
   When the set-to was done;
While ringing in the arena
   The showered denarii fell,
That told CRAWLEIUS' Novice
   Had used his mauleys well.

'Tis but some sixty years since
   The times of which I speak,
And yet the words I'm using
   Will sound to you like Greek.
What know ye, race of milksops,
   Untaught of the P.R.,
What stopping, lunging, countering,
   Fibbing, or rallying are?
What boots to use the *lingo*,
   When you have lost the *thing*?
How paint to you the glories
   Of BELCHER, CRIBB, or SPRING –
To *you*, whose sire turns up his eyes
   At mention of the Ring?

---

*An allusion to 'Gladstone claret'; cheap, thin French wines being first admitted at low duty in 1860.

†Domus Savilliana – Saville House, on the north side of Leicester Square, where sparring exhibitions and bouts were frequent.

Yet, in despite of all the jaw
    And gammon of this time,
That brands the art of self-defence –
    Old England's art – as crime,
From off mine ancient memories
    The rust of time I'll shake.
Your youthful bloods to quicken
    And your British pluck to wake;
I know it only slumbers,
    Let cant do what it will,
The British bull-dog *will* be
    The British bull-dog still.
Then gather to your grandsire's knee,
    The while his tale is told
How SAYERIUS and HEENANUS
    Milled in those days of old.

Y FYGHTE

The Beaks and Blues were watching
    Agog to stop the mill,
As we gathered to the station
    In the April morning chill;
By twos and threes, by fours and tens,
    To London Bridge we drew;
For we had had 'the office'
    That were good men and true;
And saving such, the place of fight
    Was ne'er a man that knew.
From East, from West, from North and South,
    The London Fancy poured,
Down to the sporting cabman,
    Up to the sporting lord;
From the 'Horseshoe' in Tichbourne Street
    Sharp OWEN SWIFT was there;
JEM BURN had left the 'Rising Sun',
    All in the Street of Air;
LANGHAM had cut the 'Cambrian',
    With tough old ALEC REID,
And towering high above the crowd
    Shone BEN CAUNT's fragrant weed;
Not only fighting covies,
    But sporting swells besides –
Dukes, Lords, M.P.'s, and Guardsmen,
    With county Beaks for guides;
And tongues that sway our Senators,
    And hands the pen that wield,
Were cheering on the Champions
    Upon that morning's field.

And hark! the bell is ringing,
    The engine puffs amain,
And through the dark towards Brighton
    On shrieks the tearing train;
But turning off where Reigate
    Unites the clustering lines,
By poultry-haunted Dorking
    A devious course it twines,
By Wootton, Shier, and Guildford,
    Across the winding Wey,
Till by heath-girded Farnborough
    Our doubling course we stay,
Where Aldershot lay snoring
    All in the morning grey,
Nor dreamed 'the Camp' what combat
    Should be fought here to-day.

The stakes are pitched, the ropes are rove,
    The men have ta'en their stand;
HEENANUS wins the toss for place,
    And takes the eastward hand;
CUSSICCIUS and MACDONALDUS*
    Upon 'the BOY' attend;
SAYERIUS owns BRUNTONIUS
    With JIM WELSHIUS for friend.†
And each upon the other now
    A curious eye may throw,
And from the seconds' final rub
    In buff at length they show,
And from their corners to the scratch
    Move stalwartly and slow.

Then each his hand stretched forth to grasp
His foeman's fives in friendly clasp;
Each felt his balance trim and true –
Each up to square his mauleys threw –
Each tried his best to draw his man –
The feint, the dodge, the opening plan,
Till right and left SAYERIUS tried –
HEENANUS' grin proclaimed him 'wide';
Then shook his nut – a 'lead' essayed,
Nor reached SAYERIUS' watchful head.

---

*Cusick, Heenan's trainer, and Jack Macdonald.

†Harry Brunton, host of the 'Nag's Head' at Wood Green, Jemmy Welsh, of the 'Griffin'.

At length each left is sudden flung,
    We heard the ponderous thud,
And from each tongue the news was rung,
    SAYERIUS hath 'first blood'!
Adown HEENANUS' Roman nose
Freely the tell-tale claret flows
While stern SAYERIUS' forehead shows
That in the interchange of blows
    HEENANUS' aim was good!
Again each iron mauley swung,
And loud the counter-hitting rung,
Till breathless both, and wild with blows,
Fiercely they grappled for a close;
One moment in close hug they swing,
Hither and thither round the ring,
Then from HEENANUS' clinch of brass,
SAYERIUS, smiling, slips to grass!

I trow mine ancient breath would fail
    To follow through the fight
Each gallant round's still changing tale,
    Each feat of left and right.
How through two well-fought hours and more
    Through bruise, and blow, and blood,
Like sturdy bull-dogs, as they were,
    Those well-matched heroes stood.
How nine times in that desperate mill
    HEENANUS, in his strength,
Knocked stout SAYERIUS off his pins,
    And laid him all at length;
But how in each succeeding round
    SAYERIUS smiling came,
With head as cool, and wind as sound,
As his first moment on the ground,
    Still confident and game.
How from HEENANUS' sledge-like fist,
Striving a smasher to resist,
SAYERIUS' stout right arm gave way,
Yet the maimed hero still made play,
And when 'in-fighting' threatened ill,
Was nimble in 'out-fighting,' still –
    Still did his own maintain –
In mourning put HEENANUS' glims
Till blinded eyes and helpless limbs,
    The chances squared again.
How blind HEENANUS, in despite
Of bleeding face and waning sight,
So gallantly kept up the fight,
    That not a man could say
Which of the two 'twere wise to back,

Or on which side some random crack
    Might not decide the day;
And leave us – whoso won the prize –
Victor and vanquished, in all eyes,
    An equal meed to pay.

Two hours and more the fight had sped,
    Near unto ten it drew,
But still opposed – one-armed to blind –
    They stood, those dauntless two.
Ah, me! that I have lived to hear
    Such men as ruffians scorned,
Such deeds of valour 'brutal' called,
    Canted, preached-down, and mourned!
Ah! that these old eyes ne'er again,
    A gallant mill shall see!
No more behold the ropes and stakes,
    With colours flying free!

* * *

But I forget the combat –
    How shall I tell the close?
That left the Champion's belt in doubt
    Between those well-matched foes?
Fain would I shroud the tale in night –
The meddling Blues that thrust in sight –
    The ring-keepers o'erthrown;
The broken ropes – th' encumbered fight –
HEENANUS' sudden blinded flight –
SAYERIUS pausing, as he might,
Just when ten minutes, used aright
    Had made the day his own!

Alas! e'en in those brighter days
    We still had Beaks and Blues –
Still canting rogues, their mud to fling,
On self-defence, and on the Ring,
    And fistic art abuse!
And 'twas such varmint had the power
    The Champions' fight to stay,
And leave unsettled to this hour
    The honours of that day!
But had those honours rested –
    Divided as was due,
SAYERIUS and HEENANUS
    Had cut the belt in two.

And now my fists are feeble,
  And my blood is thin and cold,
But 'tis better than Old Tom to me
  To recall those days of old.
And may you, my great-grandchildren,
  That gather round my knee,
Ne'er see worse men, nor iller times
  Than I and mine might be,
Though England then had prize-fighters –
  Even reprobates like me.

Anonymous

19th century

*Chaunt for Tom Sayers**

As we cheerlessly strayed up the path to Tom's tomb,
His memory green casts its shadows of gloom;
There's the shadow of Pride; there's the shadow of Grief,
Of Fame that's undying, of Time that's so brief;
There's the shadow of Tom striving hard to retain
Our 'blue ribbon' of might, of man's muscle and game;
There's the shadow of Death, grim Champion of all,
Had thrown down the scythe to grip Tom for a fall.
Tom evades the cold grasp; but Death, in with a plunge,
Gives the fatal cross-buttock, and throws up Tom's sponge.
Peace, peace to his manes, if we dare look above,
To the Father of mercy, compassion and love,
Test gently Tom's sins – Thy forgiveness extend
To him ever forward the weak to defend;
And though rugged and rude in some persons' esteem,
Before Thee he MAY stand – well, nearly supreme,
If his actions be squared by truth, honour and worth,
Though unaided by culture, by schoolcraft or birth.
And ye roughs, to his tomb who a pilgrimage make,
Think at the 'last trump' that 'Our Tom' shall awake;
Tread light – doff your caps – bow low o'er his bones,
And for once breathe a prayer to the Great Throne of Thrones.
And 'He who hears all men' may temper Tom's fate,
And a glorious hereafter Tom's soul may await.

*Tom Sayers, Champion of England from 1849 to 1860, died in 1866.

George Gordon, Lord Byron
1788–1824

Written After Swimming from Sestos to Abydos

If, in the month of dark December,
   Leander, who was nighly wont
(What maid will not the tale remember?)
   To cross thy stream, broad Hellespont!

If, when the wintry tempest roar'd,
   He sped to Hero, nothing loth,
And thus of old thy current pour'd,
   Fair Venus! how I pity both!

For *me*, degenerate modern wretch,
   Though in the genial month of May,
My dripping limbs I faintly stretch,
   And think I've done a feat to-day.

But since he cross'd the rapid tide,
   According to the doubtful story,
To woo, – and – Lord knows what beside,
   And swam for Love, as I for Glory;

'Twere hard to say who fared the best;
   Sad mortals! thus the gods still plague you!
He lost his labour, I my jest;
   For he was drown'd, and I've the ague.

from *The Two Foscari*

    – How many a time have I
Cloven with arm still lustier, breast more daring,
The wave all roughen'd; with a swimmer's stroke
Flinging the billows back from my drench'd hair,
And laughing from my lip the audacious brine,
Which kiss'd it like a wine-cup, rising o'er
The waves as they arose, and prouder still
The loftier they uplifted me; and oft,
In wantonness of spirit, plunging down
Into their green and glassy gulfs, and making

My way to shells and sea-weed, all unseen
By those above, till they wax'd fearful; then
Returning with my grasp full of such tokens
As show'd that I had search'd the deep: exulting,
With a far-dashing stroke, and drawing deep
The long-suspended breath, again I spurn'd
The foam which broke around me, and pursued
My track like a sea-bird. – I was a boy then.

Felicia Hemans

1793–1835

The Diver

'They learn in suffering what they teach in song.' – Shelley

Thou has been where the rocks of coral grow,
    Thou has fought with eddying waves; –
Thy cheek is pale, and thy heart beats low,
    Thou searcher of ocean's caves!

Thou has looked on the gleaming wealth of old,
    And wrecks where the brave have striven;
The deep is a strong and fearful hold,
    But thou its bar has riven!

A wild and weary life is thine;
    A wasting task and lone,
Though treasure-grots for thee may shine,
    To all besides unknown!

A weary life! but a swift decay
    Soon, soon shall set thee free;
Thou'rt passing fast from thy toils away,
    Thou wrestler with the sea!

In thy dim eye, on thy hollow cheek,
    Well are the death-signs read –
Go! for the pearl in its cavern seek,
    Ere hope and power be fled!

And bright in beauty's coronal
   That glistening gem shall be;
A star to all in the festive hall –
   But who will think on *thee*?

None! as it gleams from the queen-like head,
   Not one 'midst throngs will say,
'A life hath been like a rain-drop shed,
   For that pale quivering ray.'

Woe for the wealth thus dearly bought!
   And are not those like thee
Who win for earth the gems of thought?
   O wrestler with the sea!

Down to the gulfs of the soul they go,
   Where the passion-fountains burn,
Gathering the jewels far below
   From many a buried urn:

Wringing from lava-veins the fire
   That o'er bright words is poured!
Learning deep sounds, to make the lyre
   A spirit in each chord.

But oh! the price of bitter tears,
   Paid for the lonely power
That throws at last, o'er desert years,
   A darkly glorious dower!

Like flower-seeds, by the wild wind spread,
   So radiant thoughts are strewed; –
The soul whence those high gifts are shed
   May faint in solitude!

And who will think, when the strain is sung,
   Till a thousand hearts are stirred.
What life-drops, from the minstrel wrung,
   Have gushed with every word?

None, none! – his treasures live like thine.
   He strives and dies like thee; –
Thou, that has been to the pearl's dark shrine,
   O wrestler with the sea!

J. H. Reynolds
1794–1852

None But Himself can be His Parallel

With marble-coloured shoulders and keen eyes
Protected by a forehead broad and white,
And hair cut close lest it impede the sight,
And clenched hands, firm, and of punishing size,
Steadily held, or motion'd wary-wise,
To hit or stop – and 'kerchief drawn too tight
O'er the unyielding loins to keep from flight
The inconstant wind that all too often flies –
The Nonpareil stands. Fame whose bright eyes run o'er
With joy to see a chicken of her own,
Dips her rich pen in 'claret' and writes down
Under the letter 'R', first on the score,
'Randall, John* – Irish parents – age not known –
Good with both hands, and only ten stone four.'

To John Randall, the Famous Pugilist
In imitation of Milton's famous sonnet

Randall, whom now the envious millers own
Fighter indeed, cautious, and quick, and true
Fit to stand up with those who science knew,
The master spirits grassed by death alone;
Big Ben who made the great Tom Johnson groan,
And Pearce, who dext'rous Belcher overthrew,
Aye, and with him who turns black eyes to blue,
Cribb, negro conqueror, famous champion;
Well hast thou fought thy way to wealth and fame,
Jack Randall; and although there be who think
(For some are careless of the laurell'd brow)
But little of thy glory or thy game,
Yet when they learn that thou has touch'd the 'chink'
Some value to thy labours must allow.

*Jack Randall (1794–1828), 'The Nonpareil'.

*What is Life?**

Lines to –

And do you ask me 'what is LIFE?' –
    And do you ask me 'what is pleasure?' –
My muse and I are not at strife,
    So listen, lady, to my measure: –
Listen amid thy graceful leisure,
To what *is* LIFE, – and what *is* pleasure.
'Tis LIFE to see the first dawn stain
With sallow light the window pane: –
To dress – to wear a rough drab coat
With large pearl buttons all afloat
Upon the waves of plush: – To tie
A kerchief of the king-cup dye,
(White spoted with a small bird's eye)
Around the neck, – and from the nape
Let fall an easy fanlike cape: –
And quit the house at morning's prime,
At six or so – about the time
When watchmen, conscious of the day,
Puff out their lanthorn's rushlight ray; –
Just when the silent streets are strewn
With level shadows, and the moon
Takes the day's wink, and walks aside
To nurse a nap till eventide.
'Tis LIFE, to reach the livery stable,
Secure the *ribbons* and the *day-bill*
And mount a gig that had a spring
Some summers back; – and then take wing
Behind (in Mr. Hamlet's tongue)
A jade whose 'withers are unwrung;'
Who stands erect, and yet forlorn,
And, from a *half pay* life of corn,
Shewing as many *points* each way
As Martial's Epigrammata,
Yet who, when set a going, goes
Like one undestined to repose.
'Tis LIFE to revel down the road,
And *queer* each o'er-fraught chaise's load;
To rave and rattle at the *gate*,
And shower upon the *gatherer's* pate
Damns by the dozens, and such speeches
As well betoken one's *slang* riches

---

*In the poem the Hurst is Mousley Hurst, scene of much prizefighting; Cy Davis was known as 'The Gay Bristol Boy'; 'Gas Light Man' was the nickname of Tom Hickman; the initials P.C. denote the Pugilistic Club.

To take of Deady's bright *stark naked*
A glass or so. – 'tis LIFE to take it!
To see the *Hurst* with tents encampt on;
Lurk around Lawrence's at Hampton;
Join the *flash* crowd, (the horse being led
Into the yard, and clean'd, and fed);
Talk to Dav' Hudson, and Cy' Davis,
(The last a fighting *rara avis*,)
And, half in secret scheme a plan
For trying the hardy *Gas-light Man*.

'Tis LIFE to cross the laden ferry,
With boon companions, wild and merry,
And see the ring upon the *Hurst*
With carts encircled – hear the burst
At distance, of the eager crowd. –

Oh, it *is* LIFE! to see a proud
And dauntless man step, full of hopes,
Up to the P.C. stakes and ropes,
Throw in his hat, and with a spring
Get gallantly within the ring;
Eye the wide crowd, and walk awhile,
Taking all cheerings with a smile:
To see him strip, – his well train'd form,
White, glowing, muscular, and warm,
All beautiful in conscious power,
Relaxed and quiet, till the hour;
His glossy and transparent frame,
In radiant plight to strive for fame!
To look upon the clean shap'd limb
In silk and flannel clothed trim; –
While round the waist the kerchief tied
Makes the flesh glow in richer pride.
'Tis more than LIFE, – to watch him hold
His hand forth, tremulous yet bold,
Over his second's, and to clasp
His rival's in a quiet grasp;
To watch the noble attitude
He takes, – the crowd in breathless mood, –
And then to see, with adamant start,
The muscles set, – and the great heart
Hurl a courageous splendid light
Into the eye, – and then, the FIGHT!

Song (from *King Timms the First*)

I've had my sport at Tothill Fields,
    I've sunned myself at Gooseberry Fair;
And all the *lark* that Greenwich yields,
    Has fallen to my Easter share:
I've shy'd with stick, to win a bit
    The *backy-box* of brown japan;
And shin, and pin, and box I've hit;
    And often pitch'd, and *broke* the man!

I've loung'd at Dog-fights – noiseless scene!
    A *half-bred* betwixt calf and calf;
I've blown a gentle cloud, I ween,
    Over my gentler half-and-half!
A Bait hath given me rich delight,
    While loud would rise the rapturous shout,
When brute with brute began to fight,
    And horns were in, and bowels out!

I've watched the bruiser's winning art,
    To lure his friend into his arms;
And punch his head with all his heart,
    Commingling all the face's charms: –
I've watch'd the seconds pat and nurse
    Their man; – and seen him put to bed;
With twenty guineas in his purse,
    And not an eye within his head!

At Rowing matches have I been,
    Where naked bodies tug for coats;
And Bankside beauties have I seen,
    Sit drinking rum in little boats:
And oft on Sundays, scorning land,
    With braces loosened from the breech;
I've pull'd a girl, with blister'd hand,
    And bleeding heart, through Chelsea Reach!

Long at Fate's E O table, I
    Have play'd, and met at last a loss;
Gone *odd or even* with the sky,
    And tried the sea at *pitch and toss*: –
But all is over, – here I am, –
    My days go *five in nine* for food;
And I can have no other game,
    But playing *hazard* in a wood!

Dull Innocence! I waddle on, –
    Thy weary worshipper – and fain
Would give thee up, to be a Don,

And beat the watch in Drury Lane!
The air here feels no hats thrown up,
  His dog no costermonger catches; –
Farewell to bull, and stake, and pup, –
  And pipes, and gin, and rowing matches!

Lines to Philip Samson*

The Brummagem Youth

Go back to Brummagem! go back to Brummagem!
  Youth of that ancient and halfpenny town!
Maul manufacturers; rattle, and rummage 'em; –
  Country swell'd heads may afford you renown:
Here in Town-rings, we find Fame very fast go,
  The exquisite *light weights* are heavy to bruise;
For the graceful and punishing hand of Belasco
  Foils, – and *will* foil all attempts on the Jews.

Go back to Brummagem, while you've a head on!
  For bread from the *Fancy* is light weight enough;
Moulsey, whose turf is the sweetest to tread on,
  Candidly owns you're a good *bit of stuff*.

But hot heads and slow hands are utterly useless,
  When Israelite science and caution awake;
So pr'ythee go home, Youth! and pester the Jews less,
  And work for a *cutlet*, and not for a *stake*.

Turn up the *raws* at a fair or a holiday,
  Make you fist free with each Brummagem rib;
But never again, Lad, commit such a folly, pray!
  As sigh to be one of the messmates of Crib.
Leave the P.C. purse, for others to handle, –
  Throw up no hat in a Moulsey Hurst sun; –
Bid adieu, by the two-penny post, to Jack Randall,
  And take the outside of the coach, – one pound one!

Samson! forget that there are such men as Scroggins,
  And Shelton and Carter, and Bob Burns and Spring:
Forget *toss for sides*, and forget all the floggings, –
  While shirts are pull'd off, – to make perfect the ring.
Your heart is a real one, but skill, Phil, is wanted;
  Without it, all uselessly bravery begs: –
Be content that you've beat Dolly Smith, and been *chaunted*, –
  And train'd, – stripp'd, – and pitted, – and hit off your legs!

---

*Phil Sampson, 'The Birmingham Youth', drew with A. Belasco then defeated him (on 21 December 1820) over twelve rounds; he defeated Dolly Smith on 24 August 1819.

from *The Fields of Tothill*

Bessy the beautiful, you needs must think,
    Was not without her feelings or her suitors:
She was adored by those who are the pink
    Of that wild neighbourhood – by college tutors,
And sober serjeants: – privates too in drink,
    While pamper'd by those red kites their recruitors,
Would ope their minds, when, from the feverish drouth
Of gin and beer, they scarce could ope their mouth.

The highest in the Fancy – all the game ones
    Who were not very much beneath her weight,
Would take her ivory fingers in their lame ones,
    And woo her very ardently to mate:
But she, although she did not love the tame ones,
    Was not for men of such a desperate fate;
She knew a smart blow, from a handsome giver,
Could darken *lights*, and much abuse the *liver*.

And eyes are things that may be bung'd or blacken'ed –
    And noses may lie down upon the face –
Unless the pace of a quick fist is slacken'd;
    And jawbones will break down, to their disgrace;
And oftentimes a facer from the back hand,
    Will leave of poor Humanity no trace.
She, like a prudent woman, well reflected
On all these things, and dozens she rejected.

But many of my readers may not know
    What 'tis the *Fancy* means, so I'll explain it.
I hope the very learned will not throw
    Slurs on my explanation, and disdain it;
The best of language can be but so so –
    Tho' Berkley breed it, and tho' Barclay train it.
I struggle all I can – I do my best;
The thing is difficult – but let that rest.

Fancy's a term for every blackguardism –
    A term for favourite men, and favourite cocks –
A term for gentlemen who make a schism
    Without the lobby, or within the box –
For the best rogues of polish'd vulgarism,
    And those who deal in scientific knocks –
For bull-dog breeders, badger baiters – all
Who live in gin and jail, or not at all.

John Keats
1795–1821

Written Upon the Top of Ben Nevis

Read me a lesson, Muse, and speak it loud
    Upon the top of Nevis, blind in mist!
I look into the chasms, and a shroud
    Vaporous doth hide them, – just so much I wist
Mankind do know of hell; I look o'erhead,
    And there is sullen mist, – even so much
Mankind can tell of heaven; mist is spread
    Before the earth, beneath me, – even such,
Even so vague is man's sight of himself!
    Here are the craggy stones beneath my feet, –
Thus much I know that, a poor witless elf,
    I tread on them, – that all my eye doth meet
Is mist and crag, not only on this height,
But in the world of thought and mental might!

Anonymous
19th century

The Currie Curlers

Hurroe for the curlers, the braw Currie curlers,
    The lads that can handle the auld channel stane –
They're no very mony, but oh, they play bonnie –
    They're as gude as the best, and they're second to nane.
At morn when they muster, and staun' in a cluster
    At the head o' the road wi' their besoms in hand,
Their faces glow ruddy, with nerves firm and steady,
    Fit to draw, strike, or guard at the word o' command.

The toon's folk come waukin' up the hill busy taukin',
    They're aff to the pound and across the auld brig,
Up the Kirkgate they danner, cross Kinleith they wanner,
    They staun' on the ice and each man tak's a swig.
The rinks are next steppit, the ringcutter grippit,
    And fair bonnie circles are drawn ro'on the tee,
The rank o' the cutter gars ilka heart flutter,
    O' curlers as keen as e'er curlers can be.

An' noo they're beginnin – see Alick is rinnin'
    To gather his men, he's to play against Tom;
An' Fisher plays Palmer – loud rises the clamour,
    An' the reek rises blue frae the curlin' house lum.
Oh! isna it glorious, when cauld bitin' Boreas
    Sets his smooth slippry seal on the still water's breast,
When the curlers' stanes' rattle sets a' on their metal,
    Be he cottar, or farmer, or blue bluid o' the best.

But noo to the curlin', see Willie is hurlin'
    His stane up the howe ice wi' micht an' wi' main,
He gies't a' the pouther that lies in his shouther,
    But yet's it's a hog, and Tom loses a stane.
'Noo Jamie, my mannie, come up awfu' cannie,
    Cries Alick, 'I ken that ye're stanes are gey keen;
Keen stanes are whiles fasheous, but Jamie is cautious,
    And it lies a pat lid, faith as neat as a preen.'

Then Tom waves his besom, 'Ye never can miss him,
    He's on the tee tap, look it's just chap and lie:
Weel played, man, ye've got him,' but just when it's at him,
    A lump on the ice gars him skite awa' by.
Noo Alick is roarin' wi' accents implorin',
    For a guard on this stane that lies snug in the ring.
Oh! Bruce, man, be steady, wi' ye're broom, boys, be ready,
    Soop! soop! soop him up, men, eh! that's just the thing.

'No a stane hae we in, man, ye maun gie me ane, man,
    Cries Tam, 'oh, lie there, look, draw quiet to my kowe;
Oh! that's the curl, the best i' the worl',
    Thank ye for that ane, we lie better noo.'
Wi' his broom Alick beckoned, 'See this ane lies second,
    We maun guard him, a lazy guard, just o'er the score!
Oh! man ye come bonnie, he does na need ony,
    Up hands, let die men, there, that shuts the door.'

'There's naething to hinner me chippin' their winner,
    Cries Tom, 'just gie me the inringe o' the stane;
Ah, that's Currie curlin', at the wick he comes birlin',
    An' nips oot their winner, 'hurroe we lie ane.'
But it lies half open, and Alick is hopin',
    To lick oot the first shot and lie in himsel',
He's their winner awa', and the stan'e gane in twa,
    'Shot! shot! now,' he roars oot in triumphant yell.

Then Fisher and Palmer keep up the same clamour,
    An' the blue welkin' rings wi' their yells o' delight,
Till mirk hovers o'er them, and hame lies before them,
    Deoch-an-dorras is drank an' they a' say guid nicht.
Then horroe for the curlers, the brave Currie curlers,

The lads that can haundle the auld channel stane –
They're no very mony, but oh, they play bonnie –
They're as gude as the best, and they're second to nane.

Anonymous

19th century

The Curler's Complaint

The winter hard has noo set in,
    The snaw lies on the tree,
And curlers a' wi' cheerie hearts,
    Meet round the Curlers' Tee,
But sad affliction's heavy hand
    Is laid upon me sair,
And scenes I love so much before,
    I doubt I'll ne'er see mair.

Yet memory's eye recalls to mind,
    The rinks where aft I've been,
And love, as with the rising sun,
    Lights up each well-known scene.
Aye, bright and clear they seem to me,
    For whiles a'maist I feel
The kindly grip o' friends and foes,
    In mony a gude bonspeil.

I aften think I hear the laugh,
    Sae fu' o' hearty glee.
The hearty laugh that ne'er is heard,
    But round the Curlers' Tee.
E'en noo I think, wi' broom in hand,
    I'm sooping up the stane
That takes the end, frae foemen keen,
    Wha thocht it was their ain.

Aye, aye, I dearly loved the game,
    In days lang syne gane by,
And fain am I, but aince again,
    The slippery rink to try.
But no! to me it is denied,
    My curling days are past,
Yet still I'll fondly think o' it,
    As lang as life can last.

George Murray

1812–81

The Broom and Channel-Stane

With hound and horn o'er mountain wild
    Let huntsmen sportive stray,
By winding stream and lonely loch
    Let fishers pass the day;
But dearer far, when skies are blue,
    Is yon brave icy plain,
Where curlers meet to ply the broom,
    And wing the 'channel-stane!'

High in the lift the laverock loves
    To greet the rosy morn,
And sweet the mavis pours its lay
    From out the scented thorn;
But sweeter far than song of bird,
    Or lady's melting strain,
The music that the curler loves –
    The booming 'channel-stane'.

Oh green's the isle within the wave
    Whereon the shamrock grows;
Bright are the lands that proudly boast
    The lily and the rose;
But dearer far that rugged land
    Far in the northern main,
That claims the thistle and the heath,
    The broom and 'channel-stane'.

Anonymous

19th century

The Game of Cricket

To live a life, free from gout, pain, and phthisic,
Athletic employment is found the best physic;
The nerves are by exercise hardened and strengthened,
And vigour attends it by which life is lengthened.
                      Derry down, &c.

What conducts to health deserves recommendation,
'Twill entail a strong race on the next generation;
And of all the field games ever practised or known,
The cricket stands foremost each Briton must own.
                                        Derry down, &c.

Let dull pensive souls boast the pleasures of angling,
And o'er ponds and brooks be eternally dangling;
Such drowsy worm-killers are fraught with delight,
If but once a week they obtain a fair bite.
                                        Derry down, &c.

The cricketer, noble in mind as in merit,
A taste for oppression can never inherit,
A stranger to swindling, he never would wish
To seduce by false baits, and betray a poor fish.
                                        Derry down, &c.

No stings of remorse hurt the cricketer's mind,
To innocent animals never unkind,
The guiltless his doctrine is ever to spare,
Averse to the hunting or killing the hare.
                                        Derry down, &c.

We knights of the bat the pure ether respire,
Which, heightened by toil, keeps alive Nature's fire;
No suits of crim. con. or divorce can assail us,
For in love, as in cricket, our powers never fail us.
                                        Derry down, &c.

To every great duke and to each noble lord,
Let each fill his glass with most hearty accord;
And to all brother knights, whether absent or present,
Drink health and success from the peer to the peasant.

Walt Whitman

1819–92

The Runner

On a flat road runs the well-train'd runner.
He is lean and sinewy with muscular legs.
He is thinly clothed, he leans forward as he runs.
With lightly closed fists and arms partially rais'd.

Lewis Carroll

1832–98

The Deserted Parks (Oxford)

'Solitudinem faciunt: Parcum appelant'

Amidst thy bowers the tyrant's hand is seen,
The rude pavilions sadden all thy green;
One selfish pastime grasps the whole domain,
And half a faction swallows up the plain;
Adown thy glades, all sacrificed to cricket,
The hollow-sounding bat now guards the wicket;
Sunk are thy mounds in shapeless level all,
Lest aught impede the swiftly rolling ball;
And trembling, shrinking from the fatal blow,
Far, far away thy hapless children go.

The man of wealth and pride
Takes up space that many poor supplied:
Space for the game, and all its instruments,
Space for pavilions and for scorers' tents;
The ball, that raps his shins in padding cased.
Has wore the verdure to an arid waste;
His Park, where these exclusive sports are seen,
Indignant spurns the rustic from the green;
While through the plain, consigned to silence all,
In barren splendour flits the russet ball.

Anonymous

19th century

The Football Match

It's of a football match, my boys, delightful to be seen,
And six young rippling lads who played on Salisbury Plain.
Here's health unto those rippling lads and so the game went on.

Chorus
You rippling lads, huzza! You're sure to win the day:
You will gain the prize and you'll carry it away.

The ball has been thrown up, my boys, the game it did begin;
Good Lord, how they did kick it, more like devils than like men:
They having such a notion in kicking it along.

The ball it being thrown up, my boys, the game it did draw nigh,
Young William stuck a sharp penknife into young Jackson's thigh.
Here's health unto those rippling lads and so the game went on.

Young William aimed at the ball, it was his full intent:
But then he missed his aim and right through the goal he went.
Here's health unto those rippling lads and so the game went on.

Algernon Charles Swinburne

1837–1909

A Swimmer's Dream

November 4, 1889

Somno mollior unda

I

Dawn is dim on the dark soft water,
    Soft and passionate, dark and sweet,
Love's own self was the deep sea's daughter,
    Fair and flawless from face to feet.
Hailed of all when the world was golden,
Loved of lovers whose names beholden
Thrill men's eyes as with light of olden
    Days more glad then their flight was fleet.

So they sang: but for men that love her,
    Souls that hear not her word in vain,
Earth beside her and heaven above her
    Seem but shadows that wax and wane.
Softer than sleep's are the sea's caresses,
Kinder than love's that betrays and blesses,
Blither than spring's when her flowerful tresses
    Shake forth sunlight and shine with rain.

All the strength of the waves that perish
    Swells beneath me and laughs and sighs,
Sighs for love of the life they cherish,
    Laughs to know that it lives and dies,

Dies for joy of its life, and lives
Thrilled with joy that its brief death gives –
Death whose laugh or whose breath forgives
   Change that bids it subside and rise.

II

Hard and heavy, remote but nearing,
   Sunless hangs the severe sky's weight,
Cloud on cloud, though the wind be veering
   Heaped on high to the sundawn's gate.
Dawn and even and noon are one,
Veiled with vapour and void of sun;
Nought in sight or in fancied hearing
   Now less mighty than time or fate.

The grey sky gleams and the grey seas glimmer,
   Pale and sweet as a dream's delight,
As a dream's where darkness and light seem dimmer,
   Touched by dawn or subdued by night.
The dark wind, stern and sublime and sad,
Swings the rollers to westward, clad
With lustrous shadow that lures the swimmer,
   Lures and lulls him with dreams of light.

Light, and sleep, and delight, and wonder,
   Change, and rest, and a charm of cloud,
Fill the world of the skies whereunder
   Heaves and quivers and pants aloud
All the world of the waters, hoary
Now, but clothed with its own live glory,
That mates the lightning and mocks the thunder
   With light more living and word more proud.

III

Far off westward, whither sets the sounding strife,
   Strife more sweet than peace, of shoreless waves whose glee
   Scorns the shore and loves the wind that leaves them free,
Strange as sleep and pale as death and fair as life.
   Shifts the moonlight-coloured sunshine on the sea.

Toward the sunset's goal the sunless waters crowd,
   Fast as autumn's days toward winter: yet it seems
   Here that autumn wanes not, here that woods and streams
Lose not heart and change not likeness, chilled and bowed,
   Warped and wrinkled: here the days are fair as dreams.

IV

O russet-robed November,
    What ails thee so to smile?
Chill August, pale September,
    Endured a woful while,
And fell as falls an ember
    From forth a flameless pile:
But golden-girt November
    Bids all she looks on smile.

The lustrous foliage, waning
    As wanes the morning moon.
Here falling, here refraining,
    Outbraves the pride of June
With statelier semblance, feigning
    No fear lest death be soon:
As though the woods thus waning
    Should wax to meet the moon.

As though, when fields lie stricken
    By grey December's breath,
These lordlier growths that sicken
    And die for fear of death
Should feel the sense requicken
    That hears what springtide saith
And thrills for love, spring-stricken
    And pierced with April's breath.

The keen white-winged north-easter
    That stings and spurs thy sea
Doth yet but feed and feast her
    With glowing sense of glee:
Calm chained her, storm released her,
    And storm's glad voice was he:
South-wester or north-easter,
    Thy winds rejoice the sea.

V

A dream, a dream is it all – the season,
    The sky, the water, the wind, the shore?
A day-born dream of divine unreason,
    A marvel moulded of sleep – no more?
For the cloudlike wave that my limbs while cleaving
Feel as in slumber beneath them heaving
Soothes the sense as to slumber, leaving
    Sense of nought that was known of yore.

A purer passion, a lordlier leisure,
   A peace more happy than lives on land,
Fulfils with pulse of diviner pleasure
   The dreaming head and the steering hand.
I lean my cheek to the cold grey pillow,
The deep soft swell of the full broad billow,
And close mine eyes for delight past measure,
   And wish the wheel of the world would stand.

The wild-winged hour that we fain would capture
   Falls as from heaven that its light feet clomb,
So brief, so soft, and so full the rapture
   Was felt that soothed me with sense of home.
To sleep, to swim, and to dream, for ever –
Such joy the vision of man saw never;
For here too soon will a dark day sever
   The sea-bird's wing from the sea-wave's foam.

A dream, and more than a dream, and dimmer
   At once and brighter than dreams that flee,
The moment's joy of the seaward swimmer
   Abides, remembered as truth may be.
Not all the joy and not all the glory
Must fade as leaves when the woods wax hoary;
For there the downs and the sea-banks glimmer,
   And here to south of them swells the sea.

Andrew Lang
1844–1912

Brahma

If the wild bowler thinks he bowls,
   Or if the batsman thinks he's bowled,
They know not, poor misguided souls,
   They too shall perish unconsoled.

I am the batsman and the bat,
   I am the bowler and the ball,
The umpire, the pavilion cat,
   The roller, pitch, and stumps and all.

A Song of Life and Golf

The think they ca' the stimy o't,
    I find it ilka where!
Ye 'maist lie deid – an unco shot –
    Anither's ba' is there!
Ye canna win into the hole,
    However gleg ye be,
And aye, where'er ma ba' may roll,
    Some limmer stimies me!

    Chorus – Somebody stimying me,
            Somebody stimying me,
        The grass may grow, the ba' may row,
           Some limmer stimies me!

I lo'ed a lass, a bonny lass,
    Her lips an' locks were reid;
Intil her heart I couldna pass:
    Anither man lay deid!
He cam' atween me an' her heart,
    I turned wi' tearfu' e'e;
I couldna loft him, I maun part,
    The limmer stimied me.

I socht a kirk, a bonny kirk,
    Wi' teind, an' glebe, an' a';
A bonny yaird to feed a stirk,
    An' links to ca' the ba'!
Anither lad he cam' an' fleeched –
    A convartit U.P. –
An' a' in vain ma best I preached,
    That limmer stimied me!

It's aye the same in life an' gowf;
    I'm stimied, late an' ear';
This world is but a weary howf,
    I'd fain be itherwhere.
But whan auld deith wad hole ma corp,
    As sure as deith ye'll see
Some coof has played the moudiewarp,
    Rin in, an' stimied me!

    Chorus (if thought desirable).

Ballade of Cricket

To T. W. Lang

The burden of hard hitting: slog away!
Here shalt thou make a 'five' and there a 'four',
And then upon thy bat shalt lean, and say,
That thou art in for an uncommon score.
Yea, the loud ring applauding thee shall roar,
And thou to rival THORNTON shalt aspire,
When lo, the Umpire gives thee 'leg before', –
'This is the end of every man's desire!'

The burden of much bowling, when the stay
Of all thy team is 'collared', swift or slower,
When 'bailers' break not in their wonted way,
And 'yorkers' come not off as here-to-fore,
When length balls shoot no more, ah never more,
When all deliveries lose their former fire,
When bats seem broader than the broad barn-door, –
'This is the end of every man's desire!'

The burden of long fielding, when the clay
Clings to thy shoes in sudden shower's downpour,
And running still thou stumblest, or the ray
Of blazing suns doth bite and burn thee sore,
And blind thee till, forgetful of thy lore,
Thou does most mournfully misjudge a 'skyer',
And lose a match the Fates cannot restore, –
'This is the end of every man's desire!'

Envoi
Alas, yet liefer on Youth's hither shore,
Would I be some poor Player on scant hire,
Than King among the old, who play no more, –
'*This* is the end of every man's desire!'

Ballade of Dead Cricketers

Ah, where be Beldham now, and Brett,
   Barker, and Hogsflesh, where be they?
Brett, of all bowlers fleetest yet
   That drove the bails in disarray?
And Small that would, like Orpheus play
   Till wild bulls followed his minstrelsy?
Booker, and Quiddington, and May?
   Beneath the daisies, there they lie!

And where is Lambert, that would get
    The stumps with balls that broke astray?
And Mann, whose balls would ricochet
    In almost an unholy way
(So do baseballers 'pitch' today);
    George Lear, that seldom lent a bye,
And Richard Nyren, grave and gray?
    Beneath the daisies, there they lie!

Tom Sueter, too, the ladies' pet,
    Brown that would bravest hearts affray;
Walker, invincible when set,
    (Tom, of the spider limbs and splay);
Think ye that we could match them, pray,
    These heroes of Broad-halfpenny,
With Buck to hit, and Small to stay?
    Beneath the daisies, there they lie!

Envoi

Prince, canst thou moralize the lay?
    How all things change below the sky?
Of Fry and Hirst shall mortals say,
    'Beneath the daisies, there they lie!'

Ballade of the Three Graces

(W.G., E.M., G.F.)

In the mountains and meadows of Greece,
    In the holy, the delicate air,
When Pan was the piper of peace,
    When the satyrs were all debonair,
In the days dear to old Lempriere,
    The Graces would frolic and bound;
Our Graces are still, we declare,
    The best men in England, all round!

Though the season of midsummer cease
    The blossom of Hellas to bear,
Though the critics, a cohort of geese,
    Deny that Dame Venus is fair,
The Graces, at least, are 'all there',
    And no better bats to be found,
And at point, or at long-leg, or square,
    The best men in England, all round!

May Gilbert abide in the crease!
    And the bowling of Fred may it score!

And the slows of the coroner tease
   The colonists hugely that dare!
Go smite them, ye brethren, not spare –
   Till the glades of St. John's Wood resound
With the cheers that are surely your share,
   The best men in England, all round!

Old Glostershire, cast away care,
   And go in for a new county ground,
Green Mother of cricketers rare,
   The best men in England, all round!

A Ballade of Mourning

(The Australians at Lord's, 1878)

The glories of the ball and bat,
Alas! are unsubstantial things;
Fate lays the stoutest wicket flat,
Nor spares the game's annointed kings.
Look of these 'duck's-eggs' – ranged in strings;
Hark to that shout – a losing cheer!
Ah me! (The question soothes and stings)
Where are the scores of yester-year?

I'll wear a willow round my hat
This day of days for many springs,
And sitting where the patriarch sat,
Speed the sad hours with murmurings.
That fortune should have spread her wings
And sought the lower hemisphere,
Singing, as melancholy sings,
   'WHERE are the scores of yester-year?'

The stump of Grace is taken – pat!
Vain is the sceptre Hornby swings,
Webb, Ridley, Hearne – on this and that
The bowlers' craft destruction brings.
Fatal and strange, like stones from slings,
Are Spofforth's 'fasts', and Boyle's. Oh, dear!
Lord's with the lamentations rings,
'Where are the scores of yester-year?'

   Envoi
Prince, though I know how fortune flings
Her darts, and how they disappear,
This thought my bosom racks and wrings –
Where *are* the scores of yester-year?

James Kennedy
1848–1922

Elegy on the death of James Fleming, the Scottish athlete

Come, a' ye athletes crouse an' keen,
Frae Gallowa' to Aberdeen,
Wha like to loup or put the stane,
   Or rin a race,
Come, let the tear-drops frae your een
   Rin doun your face.

The noble Fleming's breath'd his last!
My hamely muse stands maist aghast
To mark how Fortune's cauldrife blast,
   In hapless time,
Has laid him low ere barely past
   His manly prime.

Oh, Jamie was a gallant chield
As ever stood in open field!
His stalwart, grand, heroic build,
   And honest face,
To admiration aye appeal'd
   In ilka place.

Nae pride had he like them langsyne,
When athletes maist were thought divine,
When years o' practice they'd combine,
   Wi' nae sma' scaith.
For olives on their brows to twine
   Or laurel wreath.

For though, in mony a manly feat,
Braw, buirdly chields by him were beat,
He ne'er was fash'd wi' sour conceit
   Like mony a gowk;
But wrought his wark an' gaed his gate
   Like ither fowk.

What visions rise on memory's e'e,
Wi' glints o' joyous youth to me,
When thrangin' thousands in their glee
   Cam' round the ring,
Where Jamie in his majesty
   Was like a king!

An' aye sae blythe he took a part
In ilka feat o' manly art,
Nae man, however bauld or smart,
    In lith or limb,
Could ever daunt the lion heart
    That beat in him.

O weel he liked in Lowland touns
To warsle wi' the English loons;
He didna play at ups an' douns –
    An idle trick –
But garr'd their heels flee owre their crowns
    In double quick!

At running races, short or lang,
I wat ye couldna come him wrang:
When to the hill wi' furious thrang
    They swat an fyked,
The first half-mile he let them gang
    As fast's they liked –

But fleetly hameward on the track,
When little headway they could mak',
He led the whazzlin' stragglers back
    In proud career,
Fu' fleetly springing and as swack
    As ony deer.

At caber-tossing, when the rest
Had trauchled sair an' dune their best,
Then Jamie to the final test
    Wi' power advanced –
Fierce as a cyclone in the West –
    An' owre it danc'd!

An' grand it was to ane an' a'
To see him poise the iron ba',
Then send it wi' a spring awa'
    As clean's a quoit –
While owre the lave an ell or twa
    He garr'd it skyte!

An' O, it set him aye sae weel
At Highland fling or foursome reel;
Fu' blithely he could cut an' wheel
    Wi' manly grace,
An' modest smiles aye wreath'd genteel
    On Jamie's face.

But Jamie's strength and Jamie's grace –
The pride o' Scotland's stalwart race –
Has found a lang, last resting-place
   Beyond the deep,
Where far Australia's headlands trace
   Their rocky steep.

An' though cauld death, the last o' ills,
Earth's weary care forever stills,
'Twere kind amo' the Athole hills
   To hae him laid,
Mourn'd by the murmur o' the rills,
   Row'd in his plaid.

But maybe 'yont the Southron seas,
Far aff at the Antipodes,
Like thistle-down upo' the breeze'
   The wandering Scot
May come, an' wi' a tear bapteese
   The hallowed spot.

God shield his saul in Heaven's high hame!
Few earn a braver, kindlier name;
An' though he's cross'd dark Lethe's stream
   Frae human e'e,
His memory, like a gowden dream,
   Will bide wi' me.

The Curler

Saw ye e'er a vet'ran curler
   Mourning owre a broken stane,
When the game is at the thrangest,
   Ere the hin'most shot is ta'en?

How the past comes up before him,
   Like a gleam o' gowden light!
How the present gathers o'er him,
   Like a stormy winter's night!

Doun he sits upon his hunkers –
   Lifts the pieces ane by ane;
Mourns the day he cam' to Yonkers –
   Vows he's lost a faithfu' frien'!

Doun the rink comes Davie Wallace,
   Tears o' pity in his e'e,
Vex'd an' sad his very saul is,
   Sic a waesome sight to see.

Weel he kens that throbs o' anguish
    Wring the vet'ran's heart in twa;
Davie's feelings never languish –
    Davie kens we're brithers a'.

An' he speaks him kindly – 'Saunders,
    Weel I wat you've fash aneuch;
But let grieving gae to Flanders –
    Keep ye aye a calmer sough.

Stanes will gang to crokonition,
    Hearts should never gang agee;
Plenty mair in fine condition –
    Come an' send them to the tee.'

'Wheesht!' says Saunders, 'dinna mock me –
    Cauld's the comfort that ye gie;
Mem'ries gather like to choke me
    When ye speak about the tee.

Whaur's the stane I could depend on?
    Vow my loss is hard to bear!
Stanes an' besoms I'll abandon –
    Quat the curling evermair.

Weel I mind the day I dress'd it,
    Five-an'-thirty years sin' syne,
Whaur on Ailsa Craig it rested –
    Proud was I to ca' it mine.

Owre the sea, stow'd i' the bunkers,
    Carefu' aye I strave to fend,
Little thinking here at Yonkers
    I would mourn its hinder end.

Saw ye aft how ilk beginner
    Watch'd it aye wi' envious eye?
Canny aye it chipp'd the winner: –
    Never fail'd to chap an' lie.

Ne'er ahint the hog score droopin' –
    Ne'er gaed skitin past the tee;
Skips ne'er fash'd themsel's wi' scoopin'
    When they saw my stane an' me.'

Round the ither curlers gather,
    Some lament wi' serious face;
Some insist it's but a blether –
    Aft they've seen a harder case.

Davie lifts the waefu' bodie,
    Leads him aff wi' canny care,
Brews a bowl o' reekin toddy,
    Bids him drown his sorrows there.

But his heart is like to brak aye,
    An' he granes the tither grane,
Gies his head the tither shake aye,
    Croons a cronach to his stane.

Sune the toddy starts him hoisin,
    Sune he grows anither chiel –
Glorious hameward reels rejoicin'
    Wi' his senses in a creel!

The Quoit Players

What unco chances whiles will fa'
    To ony human creature;
How, kick'd about like fortune's ba',
    We prove our fickle nature.
While ane will mourn wi' tearfu' e'e
    Some dule right unexpeckit,
Anither big wi' joy we'll see
    As bright as ony cricket.

Ae time I mind, when joyfu' June
    Had brought the wand'ring swallows,
An' sweet ilk feather'd sangster's tune
    Rang through the leafy hallows;
An' Nature wore her richest grace,
    For flow'rs and blossoms mony
Were scatter'd owre earth's smiling face,
    An' a' was blithe an' bonnie.

An' thranging frae the neib'rin toun
    Cam' mohey a cheery carl,
As crouse as claimants for a crown
    They look'd for a' the warl'.
There mony a weel-skill'd curling skip
    Cam' wi' his quoits provided;
For there, that day, the championship
    Was gaun to be decided.

An' motts were placed, an' pair an' pair
    They stript them for the battle,
An' sune the quoits glanc'd through the air,

An' rang the tither rattle.
An' sudden shouts and loud guffaws
   Cam' thick an' thrang thegither,
Confused as ony flock o' craws
   Foreboding windy weather.

An' some keep pitching lang an' dour,
   Weel-match'd an' teuch 's the widdie;
While ithers canna stand the stour,
   But knuckle doun fu' ready.
An' till 't again the victor's fa'
   Wi' keener, prouder pleasure;
While rowth o' joy swells ane an' a'
   Wi' overflowing measure.

O manly sport in open field,
   Life-kindling recreation!
Compared wi' thee what else can yield
   Sic glowing animation?
Gin feckless fules wha idly thrang
   To city balls an' theatres,
Wad tak' to thee they'd grow sae strang,
   They'd look like ither creatures.

But see – they've feckly dune their best,
   An' money a pech it's ta'en them,
Till twa are left to stand the test,
   An' fecht it out atween them; –
Twa rare auld chaps o' muckle fame,
   I wat they're baith fu' handy;
Ane muckle Willie was by name,
   The tither siccar Sandie.

Now Sandie had an unco kind
   O' silent meditation, –
A gath'ring in o' heart an' mind, –
   A rapt deliberation,
An' name daur draw a breath while he
   Stood fierce as ony Pagan,
Till whizz his weel-aim'd quoit wad flee
   Like ony fiery dragon!

But Willie – open-hearted chiel –
   He never liked to face it,
Till some tried freend wad cheer him weel,
   An' tell him whaur to place it.
An' sic a job was just the thing
   That quoiters lik'd to cherish,
An' loud they gar'd the echoes ring
   Throughout the neib'rin parish.

An' sair they battled, baith as brave
    As game-cocks fechtin' frantic;
The tae shot silent as the grave,
    The tither wild 's th' Atlantic.
An' neck an' neck they ran the race,
    At ithers' heels they rattled,
Until they reach'd that kittle place –
    The shots that were to settle 't.

An' sae it was when Sandie stood
    In breathless preparation,
Some senseless gowk in frenzied mood,
    Owrecome wi' agitation,
Yell'd out – 'O Sandie, steady now!
    Let's see you play a ringer!'
Distraction rack'd pair Sandie's pow,
    An' skill forsook his finger.

Awa' the erring quoit gaed skeugh
    Wi' wildly waublin birl,
An' owre a bare pow, sure aneuch,
    It strak wi' fearfu' dirl;
A puir newspaper chield it was,
    An' aft the fowk did wyte him
For pawning that sad saul o' his
    In scraping up an 'item'.

But fegs, to gie the deil his due,
    For facts should ne'er be slighted,
At antrin times by chance somehow
    He gar'd the wrang be righted.
An' sae when that erratic quoit
    Maist fell'd him wi' a tummle,
Awa' it bounced wi' bev'llin' skyte,
    An' on the mott played whummle.

Confusion seized baith auld an' young,
    Nae uproar could surmount it;
Some vowed the quoit was fairly flung,
    Some said they couldna count it.
The referee owned up at last
    'Twas past his comprehension;
Quo' he, 'Sic unco kittle cast
    Maun bide next year's convention.'

Then Willie aimed; while some ane, seized
    Wi' wildest quoiting clamor,
Cries 'Willie, raise your quoit, man, raise 't,
    An' strike this like a hammer!

'Twill ding auld Sandie's i' the yird,
  Ne'er let mischance defy you;
You'll win the day, yet, tak' my word,
  Gude luck will ne'er gae by you.'

Encouraged, Willie wing'd his quoit
  Fair as a rocket spinning,
While ilka ane in wild delight
  Were to the far end rinnin';
When some rough chield, in reckless speed,
  Tramp'd on his neibor's corns;
When half a dozen heels owre head
  Fell like a peck o' horns.

The quoit played thud, a murd'rous yell
  Proclaimed a new disaster;
Some cried for mercy whaur they fell,
  Some cried for dacklin' plaister.
Ane vowed the quoit had broke his back,
  Twa spak' o' waur distresses;
Anither said he got a whack
  That crack'd a pair o' glasses.

Some gabbled loud, some laugh'd like mad:
  Nae wild discordant rabble
E'er sic supreme dominion had
  Sin' at the Tower o' Babel.
But sweet accord cam' in at last,
  An' ilka honest billie
Agreed that medals should be cast
  For Sandie an' for Willie.

Like royal heroes, hame they cam'
  In glorious glee thegither,
An' pledg'd their friendship owre a dram
  O' punch wi' ane anither.
But nae like kings wha seldom care
  For chields when they've mischieved them,
They baith watch'd weel the sick an' sair,
  Till healing Time relieved them.

Lang may they thrive, while ilk ane wears
  His honors nobly earn'd;
Frae persevering pluck like theirs
  A lesson might be learn'd.
May quoiters' joys be mair an' mair,
  Unvex'd by sorrow's harrows:
Sic hearty social chaps, I swear,
  I've never met their marrows.

G. F. Grace

1850–80

Lost Ball

Batting one day at the Oval,
I was scoring and quite at ease,
And I 'placed' the bowling neatly,
Piling up twos and threes.
I know not whom we were playing
Or what was my total then
But I struck one ball of Morley's
Like the sound of a great 'Big Ben'.

It fled in the golden sunlight
Like the devil away from psalms,
And swiftly, though long-leg fielded,
It slipped like an eel through his palms,
It quieted chaff and chatter
Like loves overcoming dears,
And raised a harmonious echo
Of loud, discordant cheers.

It left the perplexed fieldsmen,
Simple as perfect geese,
And rolled away in the distance
As if it were loth to cease.

I have sought and still seek vainly
Of the lost ball a sign,
That came from the shoulder of Morley
And travelled away from mine.
It may be some man from the gas-works
Will find it in his domain;
It may be that only next season
I shall strike at that ball again.

Robert Louis Stevenson
1850–94

The Canoe Speaks

On the great streams the ships may go
About men's business to and fro.
But I, the egg-shell pinnace, sleep
On crystal waters ankle-deep:
I, whose diminutive design,
Of sweeter cedar, pithier pine,
Is fashioned on so frail a mould,
A hand may launch, a hand withhold:
I, rather, with the leaping trout,
Wind, among lilies, in and out;
I, the unnamed, inviolate,
Green, rustic rivers, navigate;
My dipping paddle scarcely shakes
The berry in the bramble-brakes;
Still forth on my green way I wend
Beside the cottage garden-end;
And by the nested angler fare,
And take the lovers unaware.
By willow wood and water-wheel
Speedily fleets my touching keel;
By all retired and shady spots
Where prosper dim forget-me-nots;
By meadows where at afternoon
The growing maidens troop in June
To loose their girdles on the grass.
Ah! speedier than before the glass
The backward toilet goes; and swift
As swallows quiver, robe and shift
And the rough country stockings lie
Around each young divinity.
When, following the recondite brook,
Sudden upon this scene I look,
And light with unfamiliar face
On chaste Diana's bathing-place,
Loud ring the hills about and all
The shallows are abandoned . . .

William Henry Drummond
1854–1907

The Great Fight

Bad luck to fight on New Year's night
An' wit' your neighbor man,
But w'en you know de reason w'y
I hit heem hard on bote hees eye,
An' kick heem till he nearly die,
I t'ink you'll understan'.

If you could see ma wife an' me
At home on Pigeon Bay,
You'd say, 'How nice dey bote agree!
Dey mus' be firse-class familee
An' go de sam' as wan, two tree,'
I know dat's w'at you say.

An' New Year's Day on Pigeon Bay,
You ought to see us den,
W'it parlor feex it up so fine,
Spruce beer an' w'isky, cake an' wine,
Cigar – an' only very bes' kin'
For treatin' all our frien'.

But on de las' New Year is pas'
De win' begin to rise,
An' snow she dreef in such a way,
W'en mornin' come, ma wife she say,
'Dere won't be many folk to-day,
Or I'll be moche surprise.'

We never see, ma wife an' me,
So quiet New Year Day,
But very happy all de sam',
An' talk a lot about de tam'
Before she come to me, ma femme,
W'ile kettle sing away.

An' as we talk, de good ole clock
Go tick, tick on de wall,
De cat's asleep upon de stair,
De house is quiet ev'ryw'ere,
An' Jean Bateese, hees image dere,
Is smilin' over all.

I buy dat leetle Jean Bateese
On Market Bonsecour,
Two dollar an' your money down,
He's fines' wan for miles aroun',
Can hardly beat heem on de town,
An' I so love heem sure.

W'at's dat I hear, but never fear,
Dere's no wan on de door?
Yass, sure enough, Joe Beliveau,
An' nearly smoder wit' de snow.
Entrez! We're glad to see you, Joe –
W'y don't you come before?

'Bonjour, Ma-dame – Camille, your femme,
She's younger ev'ry day;
I hope de New Year will be bright,
I hope de baby feel all right,
Don't wake you up too moche at night?'
An' dat's w'at Joe he say.

He's so polite it's only right
He wish heem ev'ry t'ing
Dat's good upon de worl' at all,
And geev heem two tree w'at you call
Dat fancy Yankee stuff, 'high ball,'
An' den he start to sing.

You dunno Joe? Well, you mus' know
He's purty full of life,
An' w'en he's goin' dat way – Joe,
Mus' tak' heem leetle easy, so
I don't say not'ing w'en he go
For start an' kiss ma wife.

An' up an' down dey dance aroun'
An' laugh an' mak' de fun.
For spree lak' dat, on New Year's Day,
Is not'ing moche on Pigeon Bay,
Beside he's frien' of me alway,
An' so dere's no harm done.

I lak' to know jus' how it go,
Dat w'en we feel secure
Not'ing at all is goin' wrong,
An' life is lak' a pleasan' song,
De devil's boun' to come along,
An' mak' some trouble sure.

For bimeby, Joe cock hees eye,
An' see poor Jean Bateese,
An' say right off, 'If I can't show
A better wan at home, I'll go
An' drown me on de crick below,'
So dat's de en' of peace.

Dis very day along de Bay,
Dey tell about de fight.
Never was seen such a bloody war,
On Pigeon Bay before, ba gor'!
An' easy understan' it, for
De battle las' all night.

So hard we go, dat me an' Joe
Get tire soon, an' den
We bote sit down an' tak' de res'
For half a secon', mebbe less,
An' w'en de win' come on our ches',
We start her up again.

De house is shake lak' beeg eart'quake,
De way we jump aroun',
An' people living far away,
Dey lissen hard an' den dey say,
'It's all up, sure, wit' Pigeon Bay —
She's tumble to de groun'.'

'T was bad enough, de way we puff,
But w'en de stovepipe fall,
An' all de smoke begin to tear
Right t'roo de house, an' choke de air,
An' me an' Joe can't see no w'ere,
Dat's very wors' t'ing of all.

It's not a joke, de maudit smoke —
Dat's w'at I'm tellin' you —
But sure enough it stop de fight;
It's easy killin' Joe all right,
But w'at about de wife all right
An' mebbe baby too?

A man dat's brave, should always save
De woman she's hees wife;
Dat's firse t'ing he mus' do an' w'en
I open de door, Joe's runnin' den,
As hard as he can lick, ma frien',
So all han's save hees life.

An' since de fight, dey're all polite,
Dey smile an' touch de hat,
An' say, 'I hope you're feeling purty gay,
An' no more fight on Pigeon Bay,
Or else you'll kill a man some day.'
So w'at you t'ink of dat?

Edward Cracroft Lefroy

1855–91

A Cricket-Bowler

Two minutes' rest till the next man goes in,
The tired arms lie with every sinew slack
On the mown grass. Unbent the supple back,
And elbows apt to make the leather spin
Up the slow bat and round the unwary shin, –
In knavish hands a most unkindly knack;
But no guile shelters under this boy's black
Crisp hair, frank eyes, and honest English skin.
Two minutes only. Conscious of a name,
The new man plants his weapon with profound
Long-practised skill that no mere trick may scare.
Not loth, the rested lad resumes the game:
The flung ball takes one maddening tortuous bound,
And the mid-stump three somersaults in air.

A Football-Player

If I could paint you, friend, as you stand there,
Guard of the goal, defensive, open-eyed,
Watching the tortured bladder slide and glide
Under the twinkling feet; arms bare, head bare,
The breeze a-tremble through crow-tufts of hair;
Red-brown in face, and ruddier having spied
A wily foeman breaking from the side,
Aware of him, – of all else unaware:
If I could limn you, as you leap and fling
Your weight against his passage, like a wall;
Clutch him and collar him, and rudely cling
For one brief moment till he falls – you fall:
My sketch would have what Art can never give,
Sinew and breath and body; it would live.

William Sharp

1855–1905

The Swimmer of Nemi

(The Lake of Nemi: September)

White through the azure,
The purple blueness,
Of Nemi's waters
The swimmer goeth.
Ivory-white, or wan white as roses
Yellowed and tanned by the suns of the Orient,
His strong limbs sever the violet hollows;
A shimmer of white fantastic motions
Wavering deep through the lake as he swimmeth.
Like gorse in the sunlight the gold of his yellow hair,
Yellow with sunshine and bright as with dew-drops,
Spray of the waters flung back as he tosseth
His head i' the sunlight in the midst of his laughter:
Red o'er his body, blossom-white 'mid the blueness,
And trailing behind him in glory of scarlet,
A branch of the red-berried ash of the mountains.
White as a moonbeam
Drifting athwart
The purple twilight,
The swimmer goeth –
Joyously laughing,
With o'er his shoulders,
Agleam in the sunshine
The trailing branch
With the scarlet berries.
Green are the leaves, and scarlet the berries,
White are the limbs of the swimmer beyond them,
Blue the deep heart of the still, brooding lakelet,
Pale-blue the hills in the haze of September,
The high Alban hills in their silence and beauty,
Purple the depths of the windless heaven
Curv'd like a flower o'er the waters of Nemi.

The Bather

Where the sea-wind ruffles
The pale pink blooms
Of the fragrant Daphne,
And passeth softly
Over the sward

Of the cyclamen-blossoms,
The Bather stands.
Rosy white, as a cloud at the dawning,
Silent she stands,
And looks far seaward,
As a seabird, dreaming
On some lone rock
Poiseth his pinions
Ere over the waters
He moves like a vision
On motionless wings.

Beautiful, beautiful,
The sunlit gleam
Of her naked body,
Ivory-white 'mid the cyclamen-blossoms
A wave o' the sea 'mid the blooms of the Daphne,
Blue as the innermost heart of the ocean
The arch of the sky where the wood runneth seaward,
Blue as the depths of the innermost heaven
The vast heaving breast of the slow-moving waters:
Green the thick grasses that run from the woodland,
Green as the heart of the foam-crested billows
Curving a moment ere washing far inland
Up the long reach of the sands gleaming golden.
The land-breath beareth
Afar the fragrance
Of thyme and basil
And clustered rosemary;
And o'er the fennel,
And through the broom,
It floateth softly,
As the wind of noon
That cometh and goeth
Though none hearkens
Its downy wings.
And keen, the seawind
Bears up the odours
Of blossoming pinks
And salt rock-grasses,
Of rustling seaweed
And mosses of pools
Where the rosy blooms
Of the sea-flowers open
'Mid stranded waves.
As a water-lily
Touched by the breath
Of sunrise-glory,
Moveth and swayeth
With tremulous joy,

So o'er the sunlit
White gleaming body
Of the beautiful bather
Passeth a quiver
Rosy-white, as a cloud at the dawning,
Poised like a swallow that meeteth the wind,
For a moment she standeth
Where the sea-wind softly
Moveth over
The thick pink sward of the cyclamen-blossoms.
Moveth and rustleth
With faint susurrus
The pale pink blooms
Of the fragrant Daphne.

Arthur Conan Doyle

1859–1930

A Reminiscence of Cricket

Once in my heyday of cricket,
   Oh day I shall ever recall!
I captured that glorious wicket,
   The greatest, the grandest of all.

Before me he stands like a vision,
   Bearded and burly and brown,
A smile of good-humoured derision
   As he waits for the first to come down.

A statue from Thebes or from Cnossus,
   A Hercules shrouded in white,
Assyrian bull-like Colossus,
   He stands in his might.

With the beard of a Goth or a Vandal,
   His bat hanging ready and free,
His great hairy hands on the handle,
   And his menacing eyes upon me.

And I – I had tricks for the rabbits,
   The feeble of mind or of eye,
I could see all the duffer's bad habits
   And guess where his ruin might lie.

The capture of such might elate one,
  But it seemed like some horrible jest
That I should serve tosh to the great one,
  Who had broken the hearts of the best.

Well, here goes! Good Lord, what a rotter!
  Such a sitter as never was dreamt;
It was clay in the hands of the potter,
  But he tapped it with quiet contempt.

The second was better – a leetle;
  It was low, but was nearly long-hop;
As the housemaid comes down on the beetle
  So down came the bat with a chop.

He was sizing me up with some wonder,
  My broken-kneed action and ways;
I could see the grim menace from under
  The striped peak that shaded his gaze.

The third was a gift or it looked it–
  A foot off the wicket or so;
His huge figure swooped as he hooked it,
  His great body swung to the blow.

Still when my dreams are night-marish,
  I picture that terrible smite,
It was meant for a neighbouring parish,
  Or any old place out of sight.

But – yes, there's a but to the story –
  The blade swished a trifle too low;
Oh wonder, and vision of glory!
  It was up like a shaft from a bow.

Up, up, like the towering game-bird,
  Up, up, to a speck in the blue,
And then coming down like the same bird,
  Dead straight on the line that it flew.

Good Lord, was it mine! Such a soarer
  Would call for a safe pair of hands;
None safer than Derbyshire Storer,
  And there, face uplifted, he stands.

Wicket-keep Storer, the knowing,
  Wary and steady of nerve,
Watching it falling and growing
  Marking the pace and the curve.

I stood with my two eyes fixed on it,
    Paralysed, helpless, inert;
There was 'plunk' as the gloves shut upon it,
    And he cuddled it up to his shirt.

Out – beyond question or wrangle!
    Homeward he lurched to his lunch!
He bat was tucked up at an angle,
    His great shoulders curved to a hunch.

Walking he rumbled and grumbled,
    Scolding himself and not me;
One glove was off, and he fumbled,
    Twisting the other hand free.

Did I give Storer the credit
    The thanks he so splendidly earned?
It was mere empty talk if I said it,
    For Grace was already returned.

A. E. Housman

1859–1936

To an Athlete Dying Young

The time you won your town the race
We chaired you through the market-place;
Man and boy stood cheering by,
And home we brought you shoulder-high.

To-day, the road all runners come,
Shoulder-high we bring you home,
And set you at your threshold down,
Townsman of a stiller town.

Smart lad, to slip betimes away
From fields where glory does not stay
And early though the laurel grows
It withers quicker than the rose.

Eyes the shady night has shut
Cannot see the record cut,
And silence sounds no worse than cheers
After earth has stopped the ears:

Now you will not swell the rout
Of lads that wore their honours out,
Runners whom renown outran
And the name died before the man.

So set, before its echoes fade,
The fleet foot on the sill of shade,
And hold to the low lintel up
The still-defended challenge-cup.

And round that early-laurelled head
Will flock to gaze the strengthless dead
And find unwithered on its curls
The garland briefer than a girl's.

J. K. Stephen
1859–92

Boating Song KBC

Lent 1880

(Air: *It's a fine hunting day*)

On a damp windy day
In tempestuous May,
In a most insufficient attire,
What a pleasure to row
For a furlong or so,
And to glow with a patriot's fire:
There is glory to win in the fray,
There are crowds to applaud all the way,
We shall very soon be
At the top of the tree
If we all go out every day.

   Chorus
Let's go out every day
From now till the middle of May:
We shall very soon be
At the top of the tree
If we all go out every day.

By the top of the tree,
As I think you must see,
It's the head of the river I mean:
An appropriate place
For our vessel to grace
At which she will shortly be seen:
There are still a few boats in the way,
But Rome is not built in a day,
And I have not a doubt
We shall bring it about
If we all go out every day.

Chorus

Says our captain, says he: –
'May you all of you be
Dissected and roasted and skinned:
Five rowed with his back
In the shape of a sack
And then, when I swore at him, grinned:
Six, get those hands sharper away!
Keep your eyes in the boat there, I say!
Now get on to do it, do!
Get that body down, Two!
Your time's worse than ever to-day.'

Chorus

Both our Tutors are there,
Neither pleasure nor care
Can keep them away from the scene:
And who shouteth so loud
In that jubilant crowd
As each blown but uproarious Dean?
The Provost brings down Mrs A.,
Who runs a good part of the way;
Oscar Browning himself
Throws his gown on the shelf
And dismisses his staff for the day.

Chorus

*The Hundred Yards Race**

You ask me for a prophecy
About the hundred: I reply
That man can do no more than try;
And so commence and cast about
To find the lucky athletes out.
The goddess of the football field
Some valuable hints may yield:
Inured to grisly war's alarms:
She knows of many a feat of arms,
Full many a tale has she to tell
Of those who nobly fight and well:
'Twas hers to sing the artful J.,
Whose progress nothing could delay:
'Twas hers to sing Hunt's reckless rush
Through flooded fields and slimy slush,
The while with gentle words he tried
To win like prowess from his side.
These, and a host of such as they,
She sings no longer, sad to say:
    But champions still remain
Who furnish many a glorious theme
Until the past doth almost seem
    To live in them again.
For now the warlike goddess sings,
Obedient to my questionings,
Of Douglas's unrivalled grace,
Of Elliot foremost in the race,
And Stephen's more majestic pace:
Of Chitty's meteoric flight,
And Anderson as swift as light;
Hawke's rapid swoop upon the ball,
Wellesley who never tires at all
    Whate'er of toil betide:
Macaulay's oft repeated bound,
Swift Bayley's feet that shun the ground,
    The Professorial stride:
Of Bryan Farrer fast as strong,
Of Lawrence' limbs so lithe and long,
Of Booth's wild gallop in the van,
    She sings the deathless praise:
How stoutly Polhill-Turner ran,
How Spring-Rice flashed across the field,
How Peirse was never known to yield,
    She tells in stirring lays:

---

*Stephen's parody of Scott appeared in the *Eton College Chronicle* (November 1877), hence the scholastic allusions.

She tells in frightened periods
How Ridley's steps disturbed the infernal gods.
But hold! my muse is running wild
   On this too stirring theme:
It was her weakness from a child;
Excuse it, gentle reader, pray,
Now from her eyes I dare to say
   Prophetic flashes gleam.
Put not, rash man, thy hopes in all
Who can pursue the flying ball:
Not all of these shall dare to run
When fate reserves the prize for one:
Or if it shall most kindly be
Can never favour more than three.
Not all that I have named shall strive
The deadly struggle to survive:
Smith may despise all worldly pelf,
Start others but not start himself;
And Chitty may be turned reporter
In Hundred, hurdle race and Quarter,
And with his note-book scour the plain
With Chronicle upon the brain.
Yet some will start: and now we reach
The wisdom I design to teach:
My task I quickly will dispose of,
There are but three your prophet knows of
Who may be safely backed for places
In this, the shortest of the races,
Macaulay, Lawrence, Elliot these
Are they: the order if you please
I'll leave to you, and so remain
Yours truly, till we meet again,
Poeta Etonensis qui
Stipendium meret Chronicli.

Parker's Piece, May 19, 1891

To see good *Tennis*! what diviner joy
Can fill our leisure, or our minds employ?
Not *Sylvia's* self is more supremely fair,
Than balls that hurtle through the conscious air.
Not *Stella's* form instinct with truer grace
Than *Lambert's* racket poised to win the *chase*.
Not *Chloe's* harp more native to the ear,
Than the tense strings which smite the flying sphere.
   When *Lambert boasts* the superhuman *force*,
Or splits the echoing *grille* without remorse:
When *Harradine*, as graceful as of yore,

Wins *better than a yard*, upon the floor;
When *Alfred's* ringing cheer proclaims success,
Or *Saunders volleys* in resistlessness;
When *Heathcote's service* makes the *dedans* ring
With just applause, and own its honoured king;
When *Pettitt's* prowess all our zeal awoke
Till high Olympus shuddered at the stroke;
Or, when, receiving *thirty and the floor*,
The novice *serves* a dozen *faults* or more;
Or some plump don, perspiring and profane,
Assails the roof and breaks the exalted pane;
When *vantage, five games all, the door* is called,
And Europe pauses, breathless and appalled,
Till lo! the ball by cunning hand caressed
Finds in the *winning gallery* a nest;
These are the moments, this the bliss supreme,
Which makes the artist's joy, the poet's dream.
    Let *cricketers* await the tardy sun,
Break one another's shins and call it fun;
Let *Scotia's golfers* through the affrighted land
With crooked knee and glaring eye-ball stand;
Let *football* rowdies show their straining thews,
And tell their triumphs to a mud-stained Muse;
Let *india-rubber* pellets dance on *grass*
Where female arts the ruder sex surpass;
Let other people play at other things;
The *king of games* is still the *game of kings*.

Francis Thompson

1859–1907

At Lord's

It is little I repair to the matches of the Southron folk,
   Though my own red roses there may blow;
It is little I repair to the matches of the Southron folk,
   Though the red roses crest the caps, I know.
For the field is full of shades as I near the shadowy coast,
And a ghostly batsman plays to the bowling of a ghost,
And I look though my tears on a soundless-clapping host
   As the run-stealers flicker to and fro,
     To and fro;
   O my Hornby and my Barlow long ago!

It is Glo'ster coming North, the irresistible,
  The Shire of the Graces, long ago!
It is Gloucestershire up North, the irresistible,
  And new-risen Lancashire the foe!
A Shire so young that has scarce impressed its traces,
Ah, how shall it stand before all-resistless Graces?
O, little red rose, their bats are as maces
  To beat thee down, this summer long ago!

This day of seventy-eight they are come up North against thee
  This day of seventy-eight, long ago!
The champion of the centuries, he cometh up against thee,
  With his brethren, every one a famous foe!
The long-whiskered Doctor, that laugheth rules to scorn,
While the bowler, piched against him, bans the day that he was born;
And G.F., with his science makes the fairest length forlorn;
  They are come from the West to work thee woe!

It is little I repair to the matches of the Southron folk,
  Though my own red roses there may blow;
It is little I repair to the matches of the Southron folk,
  Though the red roses crest the caps, I know.
For the field is full of shades as I near the shadowy coast,
And a ghostly batsman plays to the bowling of a ghost,
And I look though my tears on a soundless-clapping host
  As the run-stealers flicker to and fro,
    To and fro;
  O my Hornby and my Barlow long ago!

Sir Henry Newbolt

1862–1938

Vitaï Lampada

There's a breathless hush in the Close to-night –
  Ten to make and the match to win –
A bumping pitch and a blinding light,
  An hour to play and the last man in.
And it's not for the sake of a ribboned coat.
  Or for the selfish hope of a season's fame.
But his Captain's hand on his shoulder smote –
  'Play up! play up! and play the game!'

The sand of the desert is sodden red, –
   Red with the wreck of a square that broke. –
The Gatling's jammed and the Colonel dead,
   And the regiment blind with dust and smoke.
The river of death has brimmed his banks,
   And England's far, and Honour a name,
But the voice of a schoolboy rallies the ranks:
   'Play up! play up! and play the game!'

This is the word that year by year,
   While in her place the School is set,
Every one of her sons must hear,
   And none that hears it dares forget.
This they all with a joyful mind
   Bear through life like a torch in flame,
And falling fling to the host behind –
   'Play up! play up! and play the game!'

W. B. Yeats

1865–1939

At Galway Races

There where the course is,
Delight makes all of the one mind,
The riders upon the galloping horses,
The crowd that closes in behind:
We, too, had good attendance once,
Hearers and hearteners of the work;
Aye, horsemen for companions,
Before the merchant and the clerk
Breathed on the world with timid breath.
Sing on: somewhere at some new moon,
We'll learn that sleeping is not death,
Hearing the whole earth change its tune,
Its flesh being wild, and it again
Crying aloud as the racecourse is,
And we find hearteners among men
That ride upon horses.

Stephen Crane
1871–1900

'I saw a man pursuing the horizon'

I saw a man pursuing the horizon;
Round and round they sped.
I was disturbed at this;
I accosted the man.
'It is futile,' I said,
'You can never –'

'You lie,' he cried,
And ran on.

Robert Service
1874–1958

The Bruiser

So iron-grim and icy cool
I bored in on him like a bull.
As if one with the solid ground
I took his blows round after round:
Glutton for punishment am I,
Rather than quit prepared to die.

Like dancing master was the boy,
Graceful and light, a boxer's joy.
He flapped a left and tapped a right –
I laughed because his blows were light;
The gong was like a golden chime,
As darkly I abode my time.

It's hard to stand ten grilling rounds.
I saw despite his leaps and bounds
That he was tired and failing fast;
But little longer could he last,
While I as solid as a rock
Grinned and withstood shock after shock.

Round eight: I launched to the attack.
I gave him all, held nothing back,
Disdained defence, with hammer blows:
The blood was spouting from his nose;
One eye, cut open, glistened wild . . .
Sudden he seemed a helpless child.

Round nine: They'd washed the blood away.
But bang! It spouted bright and gay.
His face was all a gory mask,
And yet no mercy would he ask.
Ah yes, the boy was gallant game,
Yet I must down him all the same.

Round ten: His eye like oyster gleamed.
I could have blinded him it seemed.
Then as he weaved, faint and forlorn,
Strange pity in my heart was born.
I dropped my hands unto my side:
'For God's sake, strike me, lad!' I cried.

He struck me twice, two loving taps,
As if he understood, perhaps.
Then as the gong went like a knell,
Fainting into my arms he fell.
We kissed each other, he and I . . .
'*A draw!*' I heard the umpire cry.

John Masefield

1878–1967

The Racer

I saw the racer coming to the jump,
   Staring with fiery eyeballs as he rusht,
I heard the blood within his body thump,
   I saw him launch, I heard the toppings crusht.

And as he landed I beheld his soul
   Kindle, because, in front, he saw the Straight
With all its thousands roaring at the goal,
   He laughed, he took the moment for his mate.

Would that the passionate moods on which we ride
    Might kindle thus to oneness with the will;
Would we might see the end to which we stride,
    And feel, not strain, in struggle, only thrill.

And laugh like him and know in all our nerves
Beauty, the spirit, scattering dust and turves.

Alfred Noyes

1880–1958

The Swimmer's Race

I

Between the clover and the trembling sea
    They stand upon the golden-shadowed shore
In naked boyish beauty, a strenuous three,
    Hearing the breakers' deep Olympic roar;
Three young athletes poised on a forward limb,
    Mirrored like marble in the smooth wet sand,
        Three statues moulded by Praxiteles:
            The blue horizon rim
    Recedes, recedes upon a lovelier land,
        And England melts into the skies of Greece.

II

The dome of heaven is like one drop of dew,
    Quivering and clear and cloudless but for one
Crisp bouldered Alpine range that blinds the blue
    With snowy gorges glittering to the sun:
Forward the runners lean, with outstretched hand
    Waiting the word – ah, how the light relieves
        The silken rippling muscles as they start
            Spurning the yellow sand,
    Then skimming lightlier till the goal receives
        The winner, head thrown back and lips apart.

III

Now at the sea-marge on the sand they lie
    At rest for a moment, panting as they breathe,
And gazing upward at the unbounded sky
    While the sand nestles round them from beneath;
And in their hands they gather up the gold

And through their fingers let it lazily stream
  Over them, dusking all their limbs' fair white,
    Blotting their shape and mould,
Till, mixed into the distant gazer's dream
  Of earth and heaven, they seem to sink from sight.

IV

But one, in seeming petulance, oppressed
  With heat has cast his brown young body free:
With arms behind his head and heaving breast
  He lies and gazes at the cool bright sea;
So young Leander might when in the noon
  He panted for the starry eyes of eve
    And whispered o'er the waste of wandering waves,
      'Hero, bid night come soon!'
  Nor knew the nymphs were waiting to receive
    And kiss his pale limbs in their cold sea-caves.

V

Now to their feet they leap and, with a shout,
  Plunge through the glittering breakers without fear,
Breast the green-arching billows, and still out,
  As if each dreamed the arms of Hero near;
Now like three sunbeams on an emerald crest,
  Now like three foam-flakes melting out of sight,
    They are blent with all the glory of all the sea;
      One with the golden West;
  Merged in a myriad waves of mystic light
    As life is lost in immortality.

P. G. Wodehouse

1881–1975

Missed!

The sun in the heavens was beaming:
The breeze bore an odour of hay,
My flannels were spotless and gleaming,
My heart was unclouded and gay;
The ladies, all gaily apparelled,
Sat round looking on at the match,
In the tree-tops the dicky-birds carolled,
All was peace till I bungled that catch.

My attention the magic of summer
Had lured from the game – which was wrong;
The bee (that inveterate hummer)
Was droning its favourite song.
I was tenderly·dreaming of Clara
(On her not a girl is a patch);
When, ah horror! there soared through the air a
Decidedly possible catch.

I heard in a stupor the bowler
Emit a self-satisfied 'Ah!'
The small boys who sat on the roller
Set up an expectant 'Hurrah!'
The batsman with grief from the wicket
Himself had begun to detach –
And I uttered a groan and turned sick – It
Was over. I'd buttered the catch.

Oh ne'er, if I live to a million,
Shall I feel such a terrible pang.
From the seats in the far-off pavilion
A loud yell of ecstasy rang.
By the handful my hair (which is auburn)
I tore with a wrench from my thatch,
And my heart was seared deep with a raw burn
At the thought that I'd foozled that catch.

Ah, the bowler's low querulous mutter,
Point's loud, unforgettable scoff!
Oh, give me my driver and putter!
Henceforward my game shall be golf.
If I'm asked to play cricket hereafter,
I am wholly determined to scratch.
Life's void of all pleasure and laughter;
I bungled the easiest catch.

William Carlos Williams

1883–1963

At the Ball Game

The crowd at the ball game
is moved uniformly

by a spirit of uselessness
which delights them –

all the exciting detail
of the chase

and the escape, the error
the flash of genius —

all to no end save beauty
the eternal —

So in detail they, the crowd,
are beautiful

for this
to be warned against

saluted and defied —
It is alive, venomous

it smiles grimly
its words cut —

The flashy female with her
mother, gets it —

The Jew gets it straight — it
is deadly, terrifying —

It is the Inquisition, the
Revolution

It is beauty itself
that lives

day by day in them
idly —

This is
the power of their faces

It is summer, it is the solstice
the crowd is

cheering, the crowd is laughing
in detail

permanently, seriously
without thought

J. C. Squire
1884–1958

The Rugger Match
(Oxford and Cambridge — Queen's — December)

(To Hugh Brooks)

I

The walls make a funnel, packed full; the distant gate
Bars us from inaccessible light and peace.
Far over necks and ears and hats, I see
Policemen's helmets and cards hung on the ironwork:
'One shilling', 'No change given', 'Ticket-holders only';
O Lord! What an awful crush! There are faces pale
And strained, and faces with animal grins advancing,
Stuck fast around mine. We move, we pause again
For an age, then a forward wave and another stop.
The pressure might squeeze one flat. Dig heels into ground
For this white and terrified woman whose male insists
Upon room to get back. Why didn't I come here at one?
Why come here at all? What strange little creatures we are,
Wedged and shoving under the contemptuous sky!

All things have stopped; the time will never go by;
We shall never get in! . . . Yet through the standing glass
The sand imperceptible drops, the inexorable laws
Of number work also here. They are passing and passing,
I can hear the tick of the turnstiles, tick, tick, tick,
A man, a woman, a man, shreds of the crowd,
A man, a man, till the vortex sucks me in
And, squeezed between strangers hurting the flat of my arms,
I am jetted forth, and pay my shilling, and pass
To freedom and space, and a cool for the matted brows.
But we cannot rest yet. Fast from the gates we issue,
Spread conelike out, a crowd of loosening tissue,
All jigging on, and making as we travel
'Pod, pod' of feet on earth, 'chix, chix' on gravel.
Heads forward, striding eagerly, we keep
Round to the left in semi-circular sweep
By the back of a stand, excluded, noting the row
Of heads that speck the top, and, caverned below,
The raw, rough, timber back of the new-made mound.
Quicker! The place is swarming! Around, around
Till the edge is reached, and we see a patch of green,
Two masts with a crossbar, tapering, white and clean,
And confluent rows of people that merge and die
In a flutter of faces where the grand-stand blocks the sky.

We hurry along, past ragged files of faces,
Flushing and quick, peering for empty places.
I see one above me, I step and prise and climb,
And stand and turn and breathe and look at the time,
Survey the field, and note with superior glance
The anxious bobbing fools who still advance.

II

Ah! They are coming still. It is filling up.
It is full. They come. There is almost an hour to go,
Yet all find room, the dribbles of black disappear
In the solid piles around that empty green,
We are packed and ready now. They might as well start,
But two-forty-five was their time, and it's only ten past,
And it's got to be lived through. I haven't a newspaper,
I wish I could steal that little parson's book.
I count three minutes slowly: they seem like an hour;
And then I change feet and loosen the brim of my hat,
And curse the crawling of time. Oh body, body!
Why did I order you here, to stand and feel tired,
To ache and ache when the time will never pass,
In this buzzing crowd, before all those laden housetops,
Around this turf, under the lid of the sky?
I fumble my watch again: it is two-twenty:
Twenty-five minutes to wait. One, two, three, four,
Five, six, seven, eight: what is the good of counting?
It won't be here any quicker, aching hips,
Bored brain, unquiet heart, you are doomed to wait.
Why did I make you come? We have been before,
Struggling with time, fatigued and dull and alone
In all this tumultuous, chattering, happy crowd
That never knew pain and never questions its acts . . .
Never questions? Do not deceive yourself.
Look at the faces around you, active and gay,
They are lined, there are brains behind them, breasts beneath them,
They have only escaped for an hour, and even now
Many, like you, have not escaped; and away
Across the field those faces ascended in tiers,
Each face is a story, a tragedy and a doubt;
And the teams where they wait, in the sacred place to the right,
Are bewildered souls, who have heard of and brooded on death,
And thought about God. But this is a football match;
And anyhow I don't feel equal to thinking;
And I'm certain the teams don't; they've something better to do.
And it's half-past two, and, thank Heaven, a minute over.
We are all here now. The laggards have all booked seats
And stroll in lordly leisure along the front.
What a man! Six foot, silk hat, brown face, moustache!
What a fat complacent parson, snuggling down

In the chair there, among all his cackling ladies!
I have seen that youth before. My neighbour now
On my left shouts out to a college friend below us,
'Tommy! Hallo! Do you think we are going to beat 'em?'
My watch. Twenty-to-three. That lot went quickly;
Five minutes more is nothing; I'm lively now
And fit for a five-mile run. One, two, three, four . . .
It isn't worth bothering now, it's all but here,
Here, here; a rustle, a murmur, a ready silence,
A billowing cheer – why, here they come, running and passing,
The challenging team! By God, what magnificent fellows!
They have dropped the ball, they pause, they sweep onward again,
And so to the end. Here are the rest of them,
Swingingly up the field and back as they came,
With the cheers swelling and swelling. They disappear,
And out, like wind upon water, come their rivals,
With cheers swelling and swelling, to run and turn
And vanish; and now they are all come out together,
Two teams walking, touch-judges and referee.
And they all line up, dotted about like chessmen,
And the multitude holds its breath, and awaits the start.

III

Whistle! A kick! A rush, a scramble, a scrum,
The forwards are busy already, the halves hover round,
The three-quarters stand in backwards diverging lines,
Eagerly bent, atoe, with elbows back,
And hands that would grasp at a ball, trembling to start,
While the solid backs vigilant stray about
And the crowd gives out a steady resolute roar,
Like the roar of a sea; a scrum, a whistle, a scrum;
A burst, a whistle, a scrum, a kick into touch;
All in the middle of the field. He is tossing it in,
They have got it and downed it, and whurry, oh, here they come,
Streaming like a waterfall, oh, he has knocked it on,
Right at our feet, and the scrum is formed again,
And everything seems to stop while they pack and go crooked.
The scrum-half beats them straight with a rough smack
While he holds the ball, debonair . . . How it all comes back,
As the steam goes up of their breath and their sweating trunks!
The head low down, the eyes that swim to the ground,
The mesh of ownerless knees, the patch of dark earth,
The ball that comes in, and wedges and jerks, and is caught,
And sticks, the dense intoxicant smell of sweat,
The grip of the moisture of jerseys, the sickening urge
That seems powerless to help; the desperate final shove
That somehow is timed with a general effort, the sweep
Onward, while enemies reel, and the whole scrum turns
And we torrent away with the ball. O, I know it all . . .

I know it . . . Where are they? . . . Far on the opposite line,
Aimlessly kicking while the forwards stand gaping about,
Deprived of their work. Convergence. They are coming again,
They are scrumming again below, red hair, black cap,
And a horde of dark colourless heads and straining backs;
A voice rasps up through the howl of the crowd around
(Triumphant now in possession over all the rest
Of crowds who have lost the moving treasure to us) –
'Push, you devils!' They push, and push, and push;
The opponents yield, the fortress wall goes down,
The ram goes through, an irresistible rush
Crosses the last white line, and tumbles down,
And the ball is there. A try! A try! A try!
The shout from the host we are assaults the sky.
Deep silence. Line up by the goal-posts. A man lying down,
Poising the pointed ball, slanted away,
And another who stands, and hesitates, and runs
And lunges out with his foot, and the ball soars up,
While the opposite forwards rush below it in vain,
And curves to the posts, and passes them just outside.
The touch-judge's flag hangs still. It was only a try!
Three points to us. The roar is continuous now,
The game swings to and fro like a pendulum
Struck by a violent hand. But the impetus wanes,
The forwards are getting tired, and all the outsides
Run weakly, pass loosely; there are one or two penalty kicks,
And a feeble attempt from a mark. The ball goes out
Over the heads of the crowd, comes wearily back;
And, lingering about in mid-field, the tedious game
Seems for a while a thing interminable.
And nothing happens, till all of a sudden a shrill
Blast from the whistle flies out and arrests the game.
Half-time . . . Unlocking . . . The players are all erect,
Easy and friendly, standing about in groups,
Figures in sculpture, better for mud-stained clothes;
Couples from either side chatting and laughing,
And chewing lemons, and throwing the rinds away.

IV

The pause is over. They part from each other, sift out;
The backs trot out to their stations, the forwards spread;
The captains beckon with hands, and the ball goes off
To volleys and answering volleys of harsher cheers;
For the top of the hill is past, we course to the close.
We've a three-point lead. Can we keep it? It isn't enough.
We have always heard their three-quarters were better than ours,
If they once get the ball. They have got it, he runs, he passes,
The centre dodges, is tackled, passes in time
To the other centre who goes like a bird to the left

And flings it out to the wing. The goal is open;
He has only to run as he can. No, the back is across,
He has missed him; he has him; they topple, head over heels,
And the ball bumps along into touch. They are stuck on our line;
Scrum after scrum, with those dangerous threes standing waiting,
Threat after threat forced back; a save, a return;
And the same thing over again, till the ball goes out
Almost unnoticed, and before we can see what is done,
That centre has kicked, he has thought of the four points,
The ball soars, slackens, keeps upright with effort,
Then floats between posts and falls, ignored, to the ground,
Its grandeur gone, while the touch-judge flaps his flag,
And the multitude becomes an enormous din
Which dies as the game resumes, and then rises again,
As battle of cry of triumph and counter-cry,
Defiant, like great waves surging against each other.
They work to the other corner, they stay there long;
They push and wheel, there are runs that come to nothing,
Till the noise wanes, and a curious silence comes.
They lead by a point, their crowd is sobered now,
Anxious still lest a sudden chance should come,
Or a sudden resource of power in mysterious foes
Which may dash them again from their new precarious peak,
Whilst we in our hearts are aware of the chilling touch
Of loss, a fatal thing irrevocable,
Feel the time fly to the dreaded last wail of the whistle,
And see our team as desperate waves that dash
Against a wall of rock, to be scattered in spray.
Yet fervour comes back, for the players have no thought for the past
Except as a goad to new effort, not they will be chilled:
Fiercer and faster they fight, a grimness comes
Into shoving and running and tackling and handing off.
We are heeling the ball now cleanly, time after time
Our half picks it up and instantly jabs it away,
And the beautiful swift diagonal quarter-line
Tips it across for the wing to go like a stag
Till he's cornered and falls and the gate swings shut again.
Thirty fighting devils, ten thousand throats,
Thundering joy at each pass and tackle and punt,
Yet the consciousness grows that the time approaches the end,
The threat of conclusion grows like a spreading tree
And casts its shadow on all the anxious people,
And is fully known when they stop as a man's knocked out
And limps from the field with his arms round two comrades' necks.
The gradual time seems to have suddenly leapt . . .
And all this while the unheeded winter sky
Has faded, and the air gone bluer and mistier.
The players, when they drift away to a corner
Distant from us, seem to have left our world.
We see the struggling forms, tangling and tumbling,

We hear the noise from the featureless mass around them,
But the dusk divides. Finality seems to have come.
Nothing can happen now. The attention drifts.
There's a pause; I become a separate thing again,
Almost forget the game, forget my neighbours,
And the noise fades in my ears to a dim rumour.
I watch the lines and colours of field and buildings,
So simple and soft and few in the vapoury air,
I am held by the brightening orange lights of the matches
Perpetually pricking the haze across the ground,
And the scene is tinged with a quiet melancholy,
The harmonious sadness of twilight on willowed waters,
Still avenues or harbours seen from the sea.
Yet a louder shout recalls me, I wake again,
Find there are two minutes left, and it's nearly over,
See a few weaklings already walking out,
Caring more to avoid a crush with the crowd
Than to give the last stroke to a ritual of courtesy
And a work of intangible art. But we're all getting ready,
Hope gone, and fear, except in the battling teams.
Regret . . . a quick movement of hazy forms,
O quiet, O look, there is something happening,
Sudden one phantom form on the other wing
Emerges from nothingness, is singled out,
Curving in a long sweep like a flying gull,
Through the thick fog, swifter as borne by wind,
Swerves at the place where the corner-flag must be,
And runs, by Heaven he's over! and runs, and runs,
And our hearts leap, and our sticks go up in the air
And our hats whirl, and we lose ourselves in a yell
For a try behind the posts. We have beaten them!

V

Outside; and a mob hailing cabs, besieging the station,
Sticks, overcoats, scarves, bowler hats, intensified faces,
Rushes, apologies, voices: 'Simpson's at seven',
'Hallo, Jim', 'See you next term', 'I've just seen old Peter'.
They go to their homes, to catch trains, all over the city,
All over England; or, many, to make a good night of it,
Eat oysters, drink more than usual, dispute of the match.
For the match is all over, and what, being done, does it matter?
What happened last year? I was here; I should know, but I don't.
Next year there will be another, with another result,
Just such another crowd, just as excited.
And after next year, for a year and a year and a year,
Till customs have changed and things crumbled and all this strife
Is a dim word from the past. Why, even to-night,
When the last door has been locked, the last groundsman will go,
Leaving that field which was conquered and full of men,

With darkened houses around, void and awake,
Silently talking to the silent travelling moon:
'The day passed. They have gone again. They will die.'
To-night in the moon the neighbouring roofs will lie
Lonely and still, all of their dwellers in bed;
The phantom stands will glisten, the goal-posts rise
Slanting their shadows across the grass, as calm
As though they had never challenged an eager swarm,
Or any ball had made their crossbars quiver.
Clouds will pass, and the city's murmur fade,
And the open field await its destiny
Of transient invaders coming and going.
What was the point of it? Why did the heart leap high
Putting reason back, to watch that fugitive play?
Why not? We must all distract ourselves with toys.
Not a brick nor a heap remains, the more durable product
Of all that effort and pain. Yet, sooner or later,
As much may be said of any human game,
War, politics, art, building, planting and ploughing,
The explorer's freezing, the astronomer's searching of stars,
The philosopher's fight through the thickening webs of thought,
And the writing of poems: a hand, a stir and a sinking.
And so, no more, of the general game of the Race,
That cannot know of its origin or its end,
But strives, for their own sake, its courage and skill
To increase, till Frost or a Flying Flame calls 'Time!'
I have seen this day men in the beauty of movement,
A gallant jaw set, the form of a hero that flew,
Cunning, a selfless flinging of self into the fray,
Strength, compassion, control, the obeying of laws,
Victory, and a struggle against defeat.
I know that the Power that gave us the bodies we have,
Can only be praised by our use of the things He gave,
That we are not here to turn our backs to the sun,
Or to scorn the delight of our limbs. And for those who have eyes
The beauty of this is the same as the beauty of flowers,
And of eagles and lions and mountains and oceans and stars,
And I care not, but rather am glad that the thought will recur
That in Egypt the muscles moved under the shining skins
As here, and in Greece where Olympian champions died,
And in isles long ago, where never a record was kept.

Ezra Pound

1885–1972

For E. McC
That was my counter-blade under Leonardo Terrone,
Master of Fence

    Gone while your tastes were keen to you,
    Gone where the grey winds call to you,
        By that high fencer, even Death,
    Struck of the blade that no man parrieth;
    Such is your fence, one saith,
        One that hath known you,
    Drew you your sword most gallantly
    Made you your pass most valiantly
        'Gainst that grey fencer, even Death.

    Gone as a gust of breath
    Faith! no man tarrieth,
    '*Se il cor ti manca,*' but it failed thee not!
    '*Non ti fidar,*' it is the sword that speaks
    '*In me.*'*

    Thou trusted'st in thyself and met the blade
    'Thout mask or gauntlet, and art laid
    As memorable broken blades that be
    Kept as bold trophies of old pageantry.
    As old Toledos past their days of war
    Are kept mnemonic of the strokes they bore,
    So art thou with us, being good to keep
    In our heart's sword-rack, though thy sword-arm sleep.

    Envoi

    Struck of the blade that no man parrieth
    Pierced of the point that toucheth lastly all,
    'Gainst that grey fencer, even Death,
    Behold the shield! He shall not take thee all.

---

*Sword-rune 'If thy heart fail thee trust not in me'.

Siegfried Sassoon

1886–1967

The Extra Inch

O Batsman, rise to go and stop the rot,
And go and stop the rot.
(It was indeed a rot,
Six down for twenty-three.)
The batsman thought how wretched was his lot,
And all alone went he.

The bowler bared his mighty, cunning arm,
His vengeance-wreaking arm,
His large yet wily arm,
With fearful powers endowed.
The batsman took his guard. (A deadly calm
Had fallen on the crowd.)
O is it a half-volley or long-hop,
A seventh-bounce long-hop,
A fast and fierce long-hop,
That the bowler letteth fly?
The ball was straight and bowled him neck and crop.
He knew not how nor why.

Full sad and slow pavilionwards he walked.
The careless critics talked;
Some said that he was yorked;
A half-volley at a pinch.
The batsman murmured as he inward stalked,
'It was the extra inch'.

Eugene O'Neill

1888–1953

'I used to ponder deeply' *

I used to ponder deeply o'er
The referendum and recall.
And culled statistics evermore
About the mighty tariff wall.

*O'Neill's poem was published in 1912 and refers to the eight-game series of 8–16 October between Boston Red Sox (with Joe Wood and Tris Speaker) and New York Giants (with Rube Marquard, Christy Mathewson and Jeff Tesrau). Boston won four to three.

I followed every candidate,
Read their acceptance speeches, too,
And went to hear them all orate
'Bout what they would or wouldn't do.

As I have said, my thoughts flew high,
(They very rarely touched the ground.)
So that I was considered by
My friends as being most profound.

But truth will out; I must confess
At present I am in a fix.
Although my mind's uneasiness
Has naught to do with politics.

You tell me that the G.O.P.
Has cleaned up in the state of Maine?
Hush! hush! what matters it to me?
But, say, who'll cop that opening game?

Will Wood last out? Will Marquard blow?
Is Matty still there with the science?
Can Speaker wallop Jeff Tesreau?
In brief, which is it, Sox or Giants?

Hugh MacDiarmid

1892–1978

from *The Kind of Poetry I Want*

And, above all, a poetry
Like a billiard player
Who knows how to screw
– The gripping or clinching of the cue
At the precise moment of contact with the ball
That prevents or lessens the chance of a miscue.
Even though the cue-tip may have been properly chalked
A miscue is almost inevitable
When the cue-tip hits the ball as low down
As is necessary for a strong screw
If the cue-hold is not tightened just then.
(Imagine a heavy piece of machinery
Fixed to the floor and at a convenient distance
From the table, and from this machinery
A piston-rod with its end
Shaped and tipped like a cue.

Made to shoot out like a horizontally-held cue
And strike a cue-ball
Exactly where it must be struck
To play a screw-back stroke,
Also that it travelled two or three inches
Beyond the point where it made contact with the ball.
Clearly this steel piston-rod
Could not be deflected
Either to the right or the left
By its contact with the ball.
Nor could its point be raised or lowered.
Its rigidity would only allow it
To move backwards or forwards
In a straight line.
When you grip your cue in screw-strokes
You are really attempting to make your cue
Resemble the imaginary steel cue
Which cannot deviate
From the line on which it travels.)
There are cuemen who will tell you
That they never grip the cue
For any kind of stroke.
These players *do* grip it
For screws and for many other strokes,
But this clinching of the cue
Is an unconscious action with them.
To-day practically all professionals
And most of our great amateurs
Hold the cue in the palm of the hand.
Watch the cue hand of any first-class player
When a screw stroke of any kind
Has to be played,
And you cannot fail to notice
This gripping of the cue.
You can see this closing of the hand
Round the cue quite easily
Even if the stroke
Is quite a gentle stroke.
– This is the kind of poetry I want.

Pinwheeling poetry.

Glasgow, 1960

Returning to Glasgow after long exile
Nothing seemed to me to have changed its style.
Buses and trams all labelled 'To Ibrox'
Swung past packed tight as they'd hold with folks.

Football match, I concluded, but just to make sure
I asked; and the man looked at me fell dour,
Then said, 'Where in God's name are *you* frae, sir?
It'll be a record gate, but the cause o' the stir
Is a debate on "la loi de l'effort converti"
Between Professor MacFadyen and a Spainish pairty.'
I gasped. The newsboys came running alone,
'Special! Turkish Poet's Abstruse New Song.
Scottish Authors' Opinions' – and, holy snakes,
I saw the edition sell like hot cakes!

Charles Hamilton Sorley
1895–1915

The Song of the Ungirt Runners

We swing ungirded hips,
   And lightened are our eyes,
The rain is on our lips,
   We do not run for the prize.
We know not whom we trust
   Nor whitherward we fare,
But we run because we must
   Though the great wide air.

The waters of the seas
   Are troubled as by storm.
The tempest strips the trees
   And does not leave them warm.
Does the tearing tempest pause?
   Do the tree-tops ask it why?
So we run without a cause
   'Neath the big bare sky.

The rain is on our lips,
   We do not run for prize.
But the storm the water whips
   And the wave howls to the skies.
The winds arise and strike it
   And scatter it like sand,
And we run because we like it
   Through the broad bright land.

F. Scott Fitzgerald

1896–1940

Football*

Now they're ready, now they're waiting,
Now he's going to place the ball.
There, you hear the referee's whistle,
As of old the baton's fall.
See him crouching. Yes, he's got it;
Now he's off around the end.
Will the interference save him?
Will the charging line now bend?
Good, he's free; no, see that halfback
Gaining up behind him slow.
Crash! they're down; he threw him nicely, –
Classy tackle, hard and low.
Watch that line, now crouching waiting,
In their jerseys white and black;
Now they're off and charging, making
Passage for the plunging back.
Buck your fiercest, run your fastest,
Let the straight arm do the rest.
Oh, they got him; never mind, though,
He could only do his best.
What is this? A new formation.
Look! their ends act like an ass.
See, he's beckoning for assistance,
Maybe it's a forward pass.
Yes, the ball is shot to fullback,
He, as calmly as you please,
Gets it, throws it to the end; he
Pulls the pigskin down with ease.
Now they've got him. No, they haven't.
See him straight-arm all those fools.
Look, he's clear. Oh, gee! don't stumble.
Faster, faster, for the school.
There's the goal, now right before you,
Ten yards, five yards, bless your name!
Oh! you Newman, 1911,
You know how to play the game.

---

*This was printed in the *Newman News*, the magazine of Newman School in Hackensack, New Jersey, and was written after Fitzgerald had disgraced himself on the football field.

F. R. Higgins
1896–1941

The Old Jockey

His last days linger in that low attic
That barely lets out the night,
With its gabled window on Knackers' Alley
Just hoodwinking the light.

He comes and goes by that gabled window
And then on the window-pane
He leans, as thin as a bottled shadow –
A look, and he's gone again:

Eyeing, maybe, some fine fish-women
In the best shawls of the Coombe
Or, maybe, the knife-grinder plying his treadle,
A run of sparks from his thumb!

But O you should see him gazing, gazing
When solemnly out on the road
The horse drays pass overladen with grasses,
Each driver lost in his load;

Gazing until they return; and suddenly,
As galloping by they race,
From his pale eyes, like glass breaking,
Light leaps on his face.

Hart Crane
1899–1932

The Bathers

Two ivory women by a milky sea; –
The dawn, a shell's pale lining restlessly
Shimmering over a black mountain-spear: –
A dreamer might see these, and wake to hear
But there is no sound – not even a bird-note;
Only simple ripples flaunt, and stroke, and float, –
Flat lily petals to the sea's white throat.

They say that Venus shot through foam to light,
But they are wrong . . . Ere man was given sight
She came in such still water, and so nursed
In Silence, beauty blessed and beauty cursed.

Sir John Betjeman

1906–1984

Seaside Golf

How straight it flew, how long it flew,
   It clear'd the rutty track
And soaring, disappeared from view
   Beyond the bunker's back –
A glorious, sailing, bounding drive
That made me glad I was alive.

And down the fairway, far along
   It glowed a lonely white;
I played an iron sure and strong
   And clipp'd it out of sight,
And spite of grassy banks between
I knew I'd find it on the green.

And so I did. It lay content
   Two paces from the pin;
A steady putt and then it went
   Oh, most securely in.
The very turf rejoiced to see
That quite unprecedented three.

Ah! seaweed smells from sandy caves
   And thyme and mist in whiffs,
In-coming tide, Atlantic waves
   Slapping the sunny cliffs,
Lark song and sea sounds in the air
And splendour, splendour everywhere.

Louis MacNeice
1907–63

The Cyclist

Freewheeling down the escarpment past the unpassing horse
Blazoned in chalk the wind he causes in passing
Cools the sweat of his neck, making him one with the sky,
In the heat of the handlebars he grasps the summer
Being a boy and to-day a parenthesis
Between the horizon's brackets; the main sentence
Is to be picked up later but these five minutes
Are all to-day and summer. The dragonfly
Rises without take-off, horizontal,
Underlining itself in a sliver of peacock light.

And glaring, glaring white
The horse on the down moves within his brackets,
The grass boils with grasshoppers, a pebble
Scutters from under the wheel and all this country
Is spattered white with boys riding their heat-wave,
Feet on a narrow plank and hair thrown back

And a surf of dust beneath them. Summer, summer –
They chase it with butterfly nets or strike it into the deep
In a little red ball or gulp it lathered with cream
Or drink it through closed eyelids; until the bell
Left-right-left gives his forgotten sentence
And reaching the valley the boy must pedal again
Left-right-left but meanwhile
For ten seconds more can move as the horse in the chalk
Moves unbeginningly calmly
Calmly regardless of tenses and final clauses
Calmly unendingly moves.

John Pudney
1909–77

The Speed Boat

When the speed boat cut into winter water
We were safe from our enemies,
The spies looking sleazy,
The double agents too nice,
The Mata Haris guileless as thin ice.

We were shot of the routine melodramas
And the winter water was bold
And simple as it sprayed.
With all life's dangers far behind us
We were wonderfully afraid.

Bernard Spencer
1909–63

Table-Tennis

Because the heavy lids will not drag up
I am playing table-tennis with eyes closed,
asleep, and striking at the sound;
with what a grovelling score may be supposed.

In my dream I am tired and long to stop.
Pit-ponies, sex-fiends, gypsies' bears have found
mercy, I hope, in sleep.

                    Each thump, each kick
or chastening of my day crowds back in this
unskilful ghostly tournament of poc-pic.

I know my Opponent; Who he is I miss.
The ordeal turns wilder than before;
now serve and smash must fly through a shut door.

Norman MacCaig
born 1910

Highland Games

They sit on the heather slopes
and stand six deep round the rope ring.
Keepers and shepherds in their best plus-fours
who live mountains apart
exchange gossip and tall stories.
Women hand out sandwiches,
rock prams and exchange
small stories and gossip.
The Chieftain leans his English accent
on a five-foot crook and feels
one of the natives.

The rope ring is full
of strenuous metaphors.
Eight runners shoulder each other
eight times round it – a mile
against the clock that will kill them.
Little girls breasted only with medals translate
a tune that will outlast them
with formalised legs and
antler arms. High jumpers
come down to earth and,
in the centre
a waddling 'heavy' tries to throw
the tree of life in one straight line.

Thank God for the bar, thank God
for the Games Night Dance – even though they end
in the long walk home
with people no longer here – with exiles and deaths –
your nearest companions.

Kenneth Allott

1912–73

Lament for a Cricket Eleven

Beyond the edge of the sepia
Rises the weak photographer
With the moist moustaches and the made-up tie.
He looked with his mechanical eye,
And the upshot was that they had to die.

Portrait of the Eleven nineteen-o-five
To show when these missing persons were last alive.
Two sit in Threadneedle Street like gnomes.
One is a careless schoolmaster
Busy with carved desks, honour and lines.
He is eaten by a wicked cancer.
They have detectives to watch their homes.

From the camera hood he looks at the faces
Like the spectral pose of the praying mantis.
Watch for the dicky-bird. But, O my dear,
That bird will not migrate this year.
Oh for a parasol, oh for a fan
To hide my weak chin from the little man.

One climbs mountains in a storm of fear,
Begs to be unroped and left alone.
One went mad by a tape-machine.
One laughed for a fortnight and went to sea.
Like a sun one follows the *jeunesse dorée*.

With his hand on the bulb he looks at them.
The smiles on their faces are upside down.
'I'll turn my head and spoil the plate.'
'Thank you, gentlemen.' Too late. Too late.

One greyhead was beaten in a prison riot.
He needs injections to keep him quiet.
Another was a handsome clergyman,
But mortification has long set in.
One keeps six dogs in an unlit cellar.
The last is a randy bachelor.

The photographer in the norfolk jacket
Sits upstairs in his darkroom attic.
His hand is expert at scissors and pin.
The shadows lengthen, the days draw in,

And the mice come out round the iron stove.
'What I am doing, I am doing for love.
When shall I burn this negative
And hang the receiver up on grief?'

John Arlott

born 1914

Cricket at Worcester, 1938

Dozing in deck-chair's gentle curve,
Through half-closed eyes I watched the cricket,
Knowing the sporting press would say
'Perks bowled well on a perfect wicket.'

Fierce mid-day sun upon the ground,
Through heat-haze came the hollow sound
Of wary bat on ball, to pound
The devil from it, quell its bound.

Sunburned fieldsmen, flannelled cream,
Seemed, though urgent, scarce alive,
Swooped, like swallows of a dream
On skimming fly, the hard-hit drive.

Beyond the score-box, through the trees
Gleamed Severn, blue and wide,
Where oarsmen 'feathered' with polished ease
And passed in gentle glide.

The back-cloth, setting off the setting,
Peter's cathedral soared,
Rich of shade and fine of fretting,
Like cut and painted board.

To the cathedral, close for shelter,
Huddled houses, bent and slim,
Some tall, some short, all helter-skelter,
Like a sky-line drawn for Grimm.

This the fanciful engraver might
In his creative dream have seen –
Here, framed by summer's glaring light –
Grey stone, majestic over green.

Closer, the bowler's arm swept down,
The ball swung, pitched and darted;
Stump and bail flashed and flew;
The batsman pensively departed.

Like rattle of dry seeds in pods
The warm crowd faintly clapped –
The boys who came to watch their gods,
The tired old men who napped.

The members sat in their strong deck-chairs
And sometimes glanced at the play.
They smoked and talked of stocks and shares,
And the bar stayed open all day.

Norman Nicholson

born 1914

Old Man at a Cricket Match

'It's mending worse,' he said,
Bending west his head,
Strands of anxiety ravelled like old rope,
Skitter of rain on the scorer's shed
His only hope.

Seven down for forty-five,
Catches like stings from a hive,
And every man on the boundary appealing –
An evening when it's bad to be alive,
And the swifts squealing.

Yet without boo or curse
He waits leg-break or hearse,
Obedient in each to law and letter –
Life and the weather mending worse,
Or worsening better.

Betty Parvin
born 1916

The Hockey Field

When Autumn swings a mace that cleaves
The gathering hosts till soaking sheaves
Take root again, again I see
That scene that made a mind of me.

There was a green field long ago,
Where sodden leaves swept to and fro
And quivered in the stinging clicks
As hockey ball met fighting sticks.
I trembled as the strong and tall
Came pushing past behind that ball,
All glowing girls, all warm and gold.
Irresolute, I shook with cold
And watched, my feet and fingers numb.
As 'Goal!' they shouted, I was dumb.
No one returning, bounding by,
Received the faint heart's feeble cry.

I dreamed that I was strong and tall
And followed an enormous ball
Towards a goal of such great size
Its cross-bar vanished in the skies.
I guided it, amazed – then glad.
The watchers stamped and screamed like mad.
'Shoot, shoot!' they roared. The goal drew near.
But then I stopped. I felt no fear.
I stopped. I threw away my stick.
I said: 'This hockey MAKES ME SICK!'
And left the field where, it was plain,
I'd never be afraid again.

Gavin Ewart

born 1916

September Cricket, 1975

The rough brown grass at the end of the field
where the spectators are sitting
is dappled with dead leaves (the wind lifts
them misleadingly like butterflies, and sifts
through the dryness; summer was hard-hitting).
Quiet cricket, no drama – unless someone appealed –

but for one wasp, two flies, that grass is insect-dead.
It could be, easily, fifty
years ago – the same houses, the same church –
we can say, without benefit of research,
that time, spendthrift changer, was thrifty
and changed most of this only in the head.

The clothes of the watchers and the shapes of the cars
parked round the Common
are really the only specific outward signs
that we run our lives now on different lines
since they died at Mons, on the Somme, on
those battlefields now as remote as Mars –

and we've had our own wars, big and small.
No change in the middle
with bowlers, batsmen, overs and pads –
but apart from the players (the local lads),
a few wives and kids (this is the riddle),
almost nobody is watching this game at all!

Apart from myself, just three separate old men –
count them on the fingers
of some televisual technological hand.
Yet this is Village Cricket, you understand,
an Old English thing, that still lingers
and keeps going unfailingly, like Big Ben –

so they all wishfully hope and say.
Don't let's be elegiac,
too many people are. Even with folk lore,
it's always far better to know the score
(give up head-hunting, like the head-hunting Dyak).
Perhaps, in a sunny September, village cricket has had its day?

Jake Willis
born 1917

*Mighty Mouse**

Welcome to Tyneside, little mouse!
What did Southampton ever do
To deserve the Queen Elizabeth, *and* you?
Fleetest by far over the first five yards,
Moving before the move is even on,
Never licked until you're flattened;
Take a dive? Not you! You've better things to do.
Jack-in-the-six-yard-box, on twisted cable legs,
Sprung steel? Your blistering talent
Conjures goals from non-existent openings,
At hitherto unrecorded angles. And yet
You're never too proud to fetch and carry;
No ball is ever dead when you're around.

Vest pocket ambassador, flying the Union Jack
All over Europe, and the World;
Floating, nine feet tall when centres curl
And goalies' fists are flailing – unavailing,
As they reach, despairing, for your deflections.
No shooting star has ever scorched the park
With such determination – or such a melting smile.
No man has ever fought for England with more pride
Or more integrity. Welcome home Mighty Mouse!
Those Magpies surely need you
And your example.

*After a career with Liverpool, Hamburg (whose fans called him 'Mighty Mouse') and Southampton, Kevin Keegan was signed by Newcastle in 1982.

John Jarvis
born 1917

'The Hurricane'

The chattering dies as the players walk in,
A handshake, a nod, and a smile.
Partisan feeling is almost a sin
Earth stops in its course for a while.

The table is true and the cloth is as green
As pasture on Mid-Summer Day.
Where have they come from and what have they seen,
These giants who step out to play?

The opening frame, Alex Higgins to break,
These words have hardly been said,
Than Alex is up with the speed of a snake,
Kissed the blue and gone in off a red.

His opponent is careful and seizes his chance,
With some fine methodical play.
A push here, a nudge there and sometimes a glance,
His victory's well on its way.

He pots several blacks, an occasional pink,
Higgins' eyes have followed each shot,
Between smoking and puffing and taking a drink
He's wondering what chances he's got.

His opponent finally runs out of steam,
He's already scored fifty-eight
His victory is now much more than a dream
Higgins must swallow his fate.

Alex comes to the table with no sign of fear,
He knows just what he must do.
He can't get a red and the black is well clear,
So he snookers behind the blue.

His opponent is peering, but can't see the red,
He's been sipping his water, or gin,
Alex's snooker has left him for dead,
He doesn't know where to begin.

He misses and Alex pops up like a cork,
He's already striking the white.
He's just heard he's had a big winner at York,
It could be one hell of a night!

He puts down five reds, three blacks and a brown
He's now got his sights on the blue.
If he gets it, they'll hear it way down in the town,
In Belfast and Manchester too.

Like a crack from a gun it flies into the sack,
There's only the colours to go.
One after another right down to the black,
They fall to each hurricane blow.

Snooker's played on 'the green', and it pays to be bold,
Each click of the balls sounds like cricket.
The crowd rise as they did to the Bradman of old,
When Hurricane 'comes to the wicket'.

Walker Gibson

born 1919

Billiards

Late of the jungle, wild and dim,
Sliced from the elephant's ivory limb,
Painted, polished, here these spheres
Rehearse their civilized careers –
Trapped in a geometric toil,
Exhibit impact and recoil
Politely, in a farce of force.
For this, I utter no remorse
But praise the complicated plan
That organizes beast and man
In patterns so superbly styled,
Late of the jungle, dim and wild.

Vernon Scannell

born 1922

Mastering the Craft

To make the big time you must learn
The basic moves; left jab and hook,
The fast one-two, right-cross; the block
And counter-punch; the way to turn
Opponents on the ropes; the feint
To head or body; uppercut;
To move inside the swing and set
Your man up for the kill. But don't
Think that this is all; a mere
Beginning only. It is through
Fighting often you will grow
Accomplished in manoeuvres more
Subtle than the textbooks know:
How to change your style to meet
The unexpected move that might
Leave you open to the blow
That puts the lights out for the night.

The same with poets: they must train,
Practise metre's footwork, learn
The old iambic left and right,
To change the pace and how to hold
The big punch till the proper time,
Jab away with accurate rhyme;
Adapt the style or be knocked cold.
But first the groundwork must be done.
Those poets who have never learnt
The first moves of the game, they can't
Hope to win.
            Yet here comes one,
No style at all, untrained and fat,
Who still contrives to knock you flat.

Alan Ross
born 1922

Cricket at Brighton

At night the Front like coloured barley-sugar; but now
Soft blue, all soda, the air goes flat over flower-beds,
Blue railings and beaches; below, half-painted boats, bow
Up, settle in sand, names like Moss-Rose and Dolphin
Drying in a breeze that flicks at the ribs of the tide.
The chalk coastline folds up its wings of Beachy Head
and Worthing, fluttering white over water like brides.
Regency Squares, the Pavilion, oysters and mussels and gin.

Piers like wading confectionery, esplanades of striped tulip.
Cricket began here yesterday, the air heavy, suitable
For medium-paced bowlers; but deck-chairs mostly were vacant,
Faces white over startling green. Later, trains will decant
People with baskets, litter and opinions, the seaside's staple
Ingredients. Today Langridge pushes the ball for unfussed
Singles; ladies clap from check rugs, talk to retired colonels;
On tomato-red verandas the scoring rate is discussed.

Sussex vs Lancashire, the air birded and fresh after rain.
Dew on syringa and cherry. Seaward the water
Is satin, pale emerald, fretted with lace at the edges,
The whole sky rinsed easy like nerves after pain.
May here is childhood, lost somewhere between and never
Recovered, but again moved nearer like a lever
Turned on the pier flickers the Past into pictures.
A time of immediacy, optimism, without stricture.

Post-cards and bathing machines and old prints.
Something comes back, the inkling and momentary hint
Of what he had wanted to be, though differently now
For the conditions are different, and what we had wanted
We wanted as we were then, without conscience, unhaunted,
And given the chance must refuse to want it again.
Only, occasionally, we escape, we return where we were:
Watching cricket at Brighton, Cornford bowling through sea-scented air.

Stanley Matthews

Not often *con brio*, but *andante, andante*,
    horseless, though jockey-like and jaunty,
Straddling the touchline, live margin
    not out of the game, nor quite in,
Made by him green and magnetic, stroller
Indifferent as a cat dissembling, rolling
A little as on deck, till the mouse, the ball,
    slides palely to him,
And shyly, almost with deprecatory cough, he is off.

Head of a Perugino, with faint flare
Of the nostrils, as though Lipizzaner-like,
    he sniffed at the air,
Finding it good beneath him, he draws
Defenders towards him, the ball a bait
They refuse like a poisoned chocolate,
    retreating, till he slows his gait
To a walk, inviting the tackle, inciting it.

At last, unrefusable, dangling the ball at the instep
He is charged – and stiffening so slowly
It is rarely perceptible, he executes with a squirm
Of the hips, a twist more suggestive than apparent,
    that lazily disdainful move *toreros* term
    a Veronica – it's enough.
Only emptiness following him, pursuing some scent
Of his own, he weaves in towards,
    not away from, fresh tacklers,
Who, turning about to gain time, are by him
    harried, pursued not pursuers.

Now gathers speed, nursing the ball as he cruises,
Eyes judging distance, noting the gaps, the spaces
Vital for colleagues to move to, slowing a trace,
As from Vivaldi to Dibdin, pausing,
    and leisurely, leisurely, swings
To the left upright his centre, on hips
His hands, observing the goalkeeper spring,
    heads rising vainly to the ball's curve
Just as it's plucked from them; and dispassionately
Back to his mark he trots, whistling through closed lips.

Trim as a yacht, with similar lightness
    – of keel, of reaction to surface – with salt air
Tanned, this incomparable player, in decline fair
    to look at, nor in decline either,

Improving like wine with age, has come far –
    born to one, a barber, who boxed
Not with such filial magnificence, but well.
'The greatest of all time,' *meraviglioso*, Matthews –
    Stoke City, Blackpool and England.
Expressionless enchanter, weaving as on strings
Conceptual patterns to a private music, heard
Only by him, to whose slowly emerging theme
He rehearses steps, soloist in compulsions of a dream.

World Cup

    It is, after all, a kind
Of music, an elaborating of themes
That swell and subside, which
In the converting of open spaces
Take on a clean edge.
    A throw, a chip,
A flick, Wilson to Charlton,
To Moore, to Hunt, to Greaves –
The diagonals cross, green space is charmed.

A precise movement, balletic in ordained
Agility, with the players as if magnetised
Moving into places seemingly allotted them
– They seem from above to be pushed like counters,
And only the fluffed pass, the momentary
Crudity disconcerting as a clerical oath,
Destroys the illusion. A goal restores it.

Arms raised like gladiators, they embrace.
Human emotions swamp them, childishly even
For such protagonists of perfection.
    And involved in this mixture
Of the fallible and the dreamy,
The percussive and the lilting, they demonstrate
How art exists on many levels, spirit
And matter close-knit as strangling lianas.

Dannie Abse

born 1923

The Game

Follow the crowds to where the turnstiles click.
The terraces fill. *Hoompa*, blares the brassy band.
Saturday afternoon has come to Ninian Park
and, beyond the goalposts, in the Canton Stand
between black spaces, a hundred matches spark.

Waiting, we recall records, legendary scores:
Fred Keenor, Hardy, in a royal blue shirt.
The very names, sad as the old songs, open doors
before our time where someone else was hurt.
Now, like an injured beast, the great crowd roars.

The coin is spun. Here all is simplified
and we are partisan who cheer the Good,
hiss at passing Evil. Was Lucifer offside?
A wing falls down when cherubs howl for blood.
Demons have agents: the Referee is bribed.

The white ball smacked the crossbar. Satan rose
higher than the others in the smoked brown gloom
to sink on grass in a ballet dancer's pose.
Again, it seems, we hear a familiar tune
not quite identifiable. A distant whistle blows.

Memory of faded games, the discarded years;
talk of Aston Villa, Orient, and the Swans.
Half-time, the band played the same military airs
as when The Bluebirds once were champions.
Round touchlines the same cripples in their chairs.

Mephistopheles had his joke. The honest team
dribbles infectually, no one can be blamed.
Infernal backs tackle, inside forwards scheme,
and if they foul us need we be ashamed?
Heads up! Oh for a Ted Drake, a Dixie Dean.

'Saved' or else, discontents, we are transferred
long decades back, like Faust must pay that fee.
The Night is early. Great Phantoms in us stir
as coloured jerseys hover, move diagonally
on the damp turf, and our eidetic visions blur.

God sign our souls! Because the obscure Staff
of Hell rule this world, jugular fans guessed
the result half-way through the second half
and those who know the score just seem depressed.
Small boys swarm the field for an autograph.

Silent the Stadium. The crowds have all filed out.
Only the pigeons beneath the roof remain.
The clean programmes are trampled underfoot
and natural the dark, appropriate the rain
whilst, under lamp-posts, threatening newsboys shout.

James Kirkup

born 1923

Rugby League Game

Sport is absurd, and sad.
Those grown men, just look,
In those dreary long blue shorts,
Those ringed stockings, Edwardian,
Balding pates, and huge
Fat knees that ought to be heroes'.

Grappling, hooking, gallantly tackling –
Is all this courage really necessary? –
Taking their good clean fun
So solemnly, they run each other down
With earnest keenness, for the honour of
Virility, the cap, the county side.

Like great boys they roll each other
In the mud of public Saturdays,
Groping their blind way back
To noble youth, away from the bank,
The wife, the pram, the spin drier,
Back to the Spartan freedom of the field.

Back, back to the days when boys
Were men, still hopeful, and untamed.
That was then: a gay
And golden age ago.
Now, in vain, domesticated,
Men try to be boys again.

Michael Ivens

born 1924

Sparrow at Lords Museum

Dead sparrow at Lords
Stuffed under glass with the ball
That killed you in mid flight
(Bowled by Jehanger Khan, Cambridge, 1935),
How impressive you are
Encased for ever with your murderer.

More impressive than the photographs
Of Hobbs or Compton or W.G.
Or the show of cricket bats throughout the ages.

Reverently we peer at you in your open tomb:
M.C.C. members and their wives in tow,
Open shirted boozers from the Cricketers Bar,
Sentimental children and West Indians
Having a day off from their London bus;
Heartened we return to clap the batsmen in.

Dead sparrow encased for ever with your ball
You signify the sacrifice of Life to Art,
The sacrifice that we are glad you made:
And Doctor Grace himself has noted your small fall.

John Smith

born 1924

Advice to Swimmers

To clutch at straws is to drown surely;
Better to thresh the unpropitious waves
In mock of swimming than to go thus down.
Though the sea's deep, life's deeper; miracles may,
Before the last breath, drain the encompassing ocean;
All who fall overboard do not, therefore, drown.

But to make much of driftwood is to rely
In storm or doldrums, on a too treacherous aid;
The sodden wood, like spurious faiths, may crumble
Under the trusting hand; conceivably wiser
Would be, at the last gasp, to tread water bravely;
It is, perhaps, false wisdom to be over humble.

So may that final movement of defiance
Safe to some certain shore bring the foot down;
Auspicious omen in a vast sea of doubt.
Yet at that juncture do not pause too long;
Such solid-seeming footholds still may trick you
Being sand merely, and sand, like Time, runs out.

In such wise, at extremity of anguish,
Whatever evil of cold or cramp may assail you,
The blood grown thin, the enfeebled slow pulse dimming,
There is one precept and one precept only
That's worth a fig for truth in that deep danger:
To avoid drowning is to persist in swimming.

Philip Booth

born 1925

First Lesson

Lie back, daughter, let your head
be tipped back in the cup of my hand.
Gently, and I will hold you. Spread
your arms wide, lie out on the stream
and look high at the gulls. A dead-
man's float is face down. You will dive
and swim soon enough where this tidewater
ebbs to the sea. Daughter, believe
me, when you tire on the long thrash
to your island, lie up, and survive.
As you float now, where I held you
and let go, remember when fear
cramps your heart what I told you:
lie gently and wide to the light-year
stars, lie back, and the sea will hold you.

Kenneth Koch

born 1925

from *Ko, or A Season on Earth*

'We are the Dodgers' sang that merry band;
'This is our field, our bullpen, our delight,
Our Tampa, our spring training, and our land!
But who are you, who in the dead of night
Of anxious dreams in middle day do stand
And question us? What was it caused your fright?'
The Dodgers then subsided into silence
Like ocean birds returning to their islands.

Ko, then, returning to full consciousness,
Explained to Mr. Slater and his hitters
How baseball had been all his happiness
Since when, a tiny toddler throwing spitters
At paper lanterns, he had made a mess
Of one upon the floor, which was all glitters,
And how, established thus his skill for throwing,
His skill at playing had been ever growing.

'Let's give the kid a chance!' cried Slater, moved
By Ko's intensity, his education,
And by his trans-Pacific flight. 'We're grooved
To take another pitcher on. Tarnation!
If this kid's good, the saying will be proved
That there are stranger things in God's creation
Than any of us dreams of. Get a glove,'
He finished; and Ko looked at him with love.

Although their wives were waiting, yet the team
Went willingly out to the field again
To see the stranger pitch. As in a dream,
But not the ones he had, Ko counted ten,
Wound up, and threw the baseball with such steam
That it went through the backstop, lost till when
The field would be torn down, and lazy goats
Would ramble through it gnawing shreds of coats;

It dug into the grandstand, where it stayed.
The crowd went wild – the crowd was mostly team,
Plus several wives. The catcher, with his splayed
Brown weighty glove, first spellbound, with a scream
Fell in the dirt behind the plate and prayed;
And Slater's agitation was extreme.
'Put someone else behind the plate,' he cried,
'So that this talent may be verified!'

Another catcher came. Ko raised his torso
In a high arc, then slumped it down again,
Then raised his arm and threw with such a force (Oh
It was beautiful to see) that when
The players' screams died down, they saw that, more so
Than the first, this second ball had pen-
Etrated through the enormous blocks of wood
And made the grandstand shiver where it stood.

Slater had fainted; and the golden sun
Sent down its last warm beams upon his visage
Which lay upon the field like something one
Has splattered golden paint all over (syzyg-
Ies of manager and player that stun
Them both!). With bottled soda, for its fizzage
All shaken up, and then released to spray
The unconscious manager, came shortstop Gray.

Ko meanwhile was preparing a third ball
With glove and gesture, seeing all in ruins
The grandstand, which he thought for sure would fall
With one or two more pitches. But De Bruins,
The first-base coach, ran out and stopped him, all
Emotionally shaken by these doings,
With 'You have done enough for now.' Ko paused,
Confused by what he'd heard, and as if lost.

*

'This game is opening game, and we've exhausted
Our pitching staff! and it's the second inning!
We trail by fifteen runs . . . I fear we've lost it –
Already, Coach, the box-seat crowd is thinning . . .'
Then Slater took a penny out and tossed it.
'It's heads!' De Bruins cried. 'Oh, what a din in
My ears that crowd is making,' Slater offered.
Then both went over to third-base coach Crawford.

'I'm going to call in Ko,' said Slater. 'Yes,
I know it's dangerous; he throws too hard,
And Cincinnati's thousands cannot guess
That soon their field will be an empty yard
Covered with grandstand fragments; but unless
His name is written on each trembling card
That's held in Cincinnati hands, these buggers
Will kill us all – I've never seen such sluggers!'

To Crawford and De Bruins he indicated
The row of mighty batsmen in the dugout –
Rizitznikov, whose mighty club was weighted

With steel; Valcowsky, who could pull the rug out
From under any pitcher, and, elated,
As easily as you can pull a plug out,
Could dash the fence to splinters. Both were dressed
In orange uniforms with a red vest,

A special privilege granted by the Redleg
Management to such great hitters. Gostoff,
Who made the centerfielders fall as dead, leg
Broken, all a-sprawling; Iznivrostov,
Who swung his club as though it were a lead leg
And hit the pill so hard that it was lost off
In Cincinnati's farther reaches; Bensky,
Who tripled every day; and dread Mischensky.

To these were added Broczd and Zagar Miktsin,
Of medium build, but deadly with the stick
That made the ball fly farther than a pigeon
That goes to seek its mate; so red, so thick,
So rising from their yellow shirts like pigskin,
These players' necks alone made pitchers sick,
Because they signified what strength they bore;
Over their yellow they blue jackets wore;

Their shoes were red, and on their caps was scrawled
'REDLEGS,' which meant, 'You haven't got a chance.'
At this array of strength, Slater, appalled,
Although since Florida a very dance
Of contradictions in his mind was walled
On when and whether he'd use Ko, as France
Is close to Spain, at once decided 'Yes!'
Ko, beckoned to, at heights of happiness,

Can scarcely feel the field, the mount, the ball
That's put into his hands: all seems imaginary –
The crowd, the stands, the shortstop, Slater, all;
And cannot speak, nay, no more than a badger, nary
A word, but, speechless, sees the batter fall,
The catcher, then the umpire, and like pageant airy
The infield boxes and their steel supports
At his first pitch, which as gun reports

Made a great crash. And then, from 'neath the stands
Where Ko's pitch penetrated, he sees stagger
A gray-haired man, who often with his hands
Daubs at his head, where, as if by a dagger
Struck and then struck again, blood spurts and lands
Upon the diamond. 'I am very bad hurt,'
He cries, and while the players gather round
From outfield, bullpen, dugout, base, and mound

He tells them all his story. 'I am Higby,
The famous catcher . . . Yes, I know that I
Supposedly am dead, stung by a big bee
Upon the heart, while chasing a foul fly
In 1936, but if you dig me
Up in the cemetery where I lie,
Supposedly, you'll find I am not there.
A country doctor, good at heart repair,

Chanced in to see me when I had been given
Completely up for lost, my face all covered
With a white sheet, on which a nurse had written
'THIS ONE TO CEMETERY – NOT RECOVERED,'
And, pulling back my sheet, said 'One can live in
That body still,' and, going forth, discovered
A body in the hall he substituted
For me, and took me where he'd instituted

A little clinic in the country, by
A rushing brook, with haystacks all around.
There, underneath a peaceful blue-white sky,
The doctor tended me till I was sound.
I scarcely even now could tell you why . . .
But I awoke one day and heard the sound
Of sparrows in the meadow and of robins
And of the merry farmwife spinning bobbins,

And knew that I was well again. I leaped
From where I lay, to seek my uniform
There where it hung inside a cupboard steeped
In mothballs, with its gay cuneiform
Of stitching 'round the waist, and then I heaped
A stack of bills upon the desk, and, warm
With my new liberty, ran down the stairway
To thank my benefactors for the fair way

In which they'd treated me, planning, of course,
To go immediately back to baseball.
I found the doctor riding on a horse
About the farmyard. But I saw his face fall,
Which had been brightened at my new-found force,
When I informed him of my plans. O ace ball-
Players, listen to what happened then,
And sympathize, as you are thinking men.

The doctor had a daughter, just sixteen,
Who, unbeknownst to me, while I had writhed
Upon the sickbed, cared for me – O Jean,
I see you still, I hear your father's cry, 'The d-
Urned fool's not worth it, Jean!' I see the mean

Face of your mother, from whose heart I'd scythed
Her only crop of joy: for Jean had desperately
Fallen in love with me. Her parents successfully

Persuaded her to ask me not to go
Back into ball, but stay there on the farm –
Thus they'd not lose their daughter. But my *no*
Was final, absolute! I saw no harm
In hogs and hay, in teaching things to grow,
Then cutting and burning them to keep us warm
And killing and cooking them to make us fat;
I loved the farmer's life – it wasn't that,

But that there was no smell of leather mitts,
No baseball insides all flag-coloured string,
No fences, no place where the manager sits
With nervous hands, no plate, no anything
That makes a man a hitter when he hits
And not a lousy rowdy. Though they wring
Their hands and oil their shotguns, I depart,
And Jean comes running after – oh, my heart . . . !'

The old man staggers; and they carry him
Out to the mound, where, supine, he resumes
His too-soon-ended tale: 'Her father, grim
With resolution, shot two times – two booms
I heard – but strikes his Jean though me he limn.
Insane with grief, he built a pair of tombs,
Put Jean in one, and in the other shut
Himself, to die when oxygen was not.

I vainly pounded on his tomb, insisting
That one death was enough, yet came no answer
From out that sepulchre, whose columns, twisting
As high as trees, held, trembling like a dancer,
The mother, clinging there, who in the misting
Of woody afternoons shrieked, "Yours this cancer,
This death, this hell!" I fled, and wandered for
Five years, as one who's crazed, and five years more

I walked the seashore, and for six in addition
I stood on sidewalks staring at the curb;
Till, finally, by some inward strange volition,
I drifted toward this field. I plucked an herb
That grows outside; and from the strange position,
Perhaps, of bending, felt strange thoughts perturb
My thereto deadened mind. All became clear . . .
I burrowed in and built a cottage here –'

He beckoned toward the grandstand now in part
Destroyed by Ko's first pitch – 'where I could watch
Some games, at least, until my sick old heart
Should stop, which now I fear –' Then with a swatch
Of linen came the water boy with art
To dress and bind, and wound his bloody splotch
Three times about it, and gave him water,
The man who'd loved the country doctor's daughter.

The crowd was meanwhile totally enraged
At the immense delay and at the ruins
The infield boxes were reduced to. Aged,
It seemed, by twenty years, Ko held De Bruins
And wept and seemed to faint. De Bruins gauged
What Ko was feeling and he said, 'You new ones
Are all alike. You think you hurt old Higby.
He does this every year. He wears a wig be-

Cause he has no hair at all beneath
The wig he wears because he has no hair.'
Ko smiled for the first time: his sparkling teeth
Were like white stars in light night summer air.
'Is that the truth?' he said. As in a sheath
His slim young body fitted without compare
In his red baseball suit; his hair was black;
And he was wet with tears both front and back.

'No,' said De Bruins, 'I have never seen
Higby before,' but oh, he spoke it softly.
'I said it but to comfort you . . . I mean,
The old guy's going to be all right – young Croftly,
The water boy, has' bound his head . . .' and mean-
While Slater shouted to them, 'Is it awfully
Important that you talk? Let us continue
The game, dear Ko, for if you want to win, you

Have got to do it before one A.M.'
Ko took the hill, his hands with rosin stained
All blue, which, mixed with tears, from rubbing them
Across his face, wet as if it had rained,
Stained his suit purple where he touched it – clem-
Ency, you make us change our hue! – while, pained
And anxious, he looked often at the bench
But saw no Higby, and his heart was wrenched.

Valcowsky now assumes his mighty stance;
Mischensky is on deck; Rizitznikov
Is in the hole, and one great foot he plants
Outside the dugout, cries, 'Valcowsky, shove!'
Mischensky hitches up his yellow pants,

And then his azure jacket he doth doff,
Revealing horrid muscles, twist on twist,
That writhe with every movement of his wrist.

Ko looked again for the old catcher, whom
At last he saw come out, in layers of bandages,
From inside Dodger dugout dressing room
Where he'd been washed and given cake and sandwiches
And dressed up in a Dodger-pink costume;
And of his taping one of the advantages
Was that one eye was free, so he could wink.
He winked at Ko, who felt his heart then sink

No more, but rise as to a small plateau
Where there is housing, water, and some women.
Distracted by the change, Ko pitched one low.
The next he threw as straight as a persimmon –
Valcowsky whacked it for a mighty blow
That would have hit the lights and made it dim in
The park if there had been lights on: the fence
Watched it fly over with indifference.

'O Ko,' cried Slater, rushing from the bench,
'Why did you throw so softly those two pitches?'
'To be a good man, that is the essenti-
Al thing,' Ko murmured. Slater plucked his stitches.
'You haven't gone and fallen for some wench,
Have you?' he queried. Ko looked at the niches
Far, far up in the grandstand. 'No,' he said.
It was because he'd hurt the old man's head . . .

*

To Cincinnati, though, I feel compelled,
To start my canto, since a sort of promise
Was made that, when confusion'd been dispelled
And in their seats had settled kids and mommas
To see the game again, to see who felled
Who and who felled who felled who – quick as commas
The fielders on the field – that we'd return
To Redleg Field to see the ball game burn.

Besides, Ko's reputation is at stake,
A source of great concern to those who know him.
What starting pitcher ever had worse break
Than Ko's, in hitting Higby, which did show him
The responsibility he had to take
For his fast pitching talent! Would it slow him?
This was the question dominating Slater
And all the fans, to whom the vendors cater.

Meanwhile to the University of Japan
A cable had been sent, explaining things,
And asking for encouragement; and Dan,
The clubhouse boy, into the clubhouse brings
A message reading *Ton wai yakki san*
Three hours later. Slater on the wings
Of hope flies quickly out to sleeping Ko,
Reads him the note, and sees him rise to throw!

'What does it mean?' asked Higby, when Slater told
The story in the dugout. 'Can you understand
The Japanese language?' Slater merely rolled
His eyes, and gestured with his gloveless hand
Out toward the mound. 'I read it to him cold;
It worked. That's all I need to know – it's grand!'
But what was in the message Ko well knew
And why he pitched beneath the sky's clear blue.

The entire student body of the University
Had cabled to him their encouragement;
Inyaga, whose intemperate perversity
Had made Ko groan, now joined the Dodger management
In hoping he'd wake up and with a diversity
Of pitches expose the Redlegs to the disparagement
Of all true fans, humiliated with strikeouts.
'I'll pitch,' Ko sighed, 'and I'll have no more blackouts.'

And then, for one or another reason, he thought
Of that first day in Tampa, when he'd come,
An untried stranger, in a ball hat bought
Ten thousand miles away, and how the hum
Of the Dodgers' playing had crept in, unsought,
The dreams he had in the bullpen; and the strum
Of his heart when Slater had said, 'Let's give the kid
A chance.' 'I'll do whatever I am bid,'

He thought; 'I'm grateful to them. Just as long
As Higby shows that he's to health returning,
I'll pitch my fastball. Stinting would be wrong
When all these men for victory are burning –
Slater, De Bruins, Cooper, and De Jong,
And countless others – and my friends are yearning
In far Japan for a personal victory
For all of them, as symbolized in me.'

And so he threw. And if he looked at Higby
Occasionally, it was but as one
Who looks up from his hoeing at the figtree
And smiles, and wipes his brow, and in the sun
Continues hoeing. Soon a Dodger victory

Seemed almost certain, for each Redleg gun
At Ko's swift mastery lapsed into silence;
And in the field, unnerved by the pitches' violence,

They all made errors, so that by the end
Of inning number four the score was tie –
Sixteen sixteen. Then Dodger friend on friend
Came to the plate and either lofted high
The ball until to Vine Street it did wend,
Or else hit low, when fielders with a cry
Would leap away. How many times the plate
Was crossed is too fatiguing to relate.

The Dodgers won, of course. The game was called
At one A.M., although the Reds protested,
Justly, perhaps, that the Dodger team had stalled
For over three hours and thus had manifested
An anti-sporting spirit; that they had mauled
A poor old catcher, poisoned an umpire, and divested
Another of his senses by serum, and thus deserved
To lose the game. But the Dodger win was conserved

Temporarily, at least, and oh, next morning
The Dodgers had a beautiful One-Nothing
Against their name, although it was a warning
Against too much unwarranted chest-puffing
That four teams had the same; but it was charming
To see the *one*, the *zero*, and with loving
Attention to be looking at them still
When noontide sunlight did your chamber fill,

And walk out in the street, if you were Ko,
And feel the buildings beating with a heart
That knew you, knew you! and to watch the slow
Movement of the streetcars, where, apart,
They climbed upon the hill, and then to go
With burning face out to some park where art
Has ordered nature – Eden Park, for example –
And see Kentucky, where the gamblers trample;

Then climb to Clifton, where the dazzling sun
Beats down upon you 'mid the drugstores, and
Past campus grasses till you come to one
Of the streets which leads to Vine Street, which, with grand
Bravura and agility, seems to run,
Irrespective of the way the town was planned,
From in the center to bright Clifton hill –
Plain German houses and a dark slum chill.

Maxine Kumin

born 1925

400-Meter Freestyle

THE GUN full swing the swimmer catapults and cracks
                                                        s
                                                           i
                                                         x
feet away onto that perfect glass he catches at
a
n
d
throws behind him scoop after scoop cunningly moving
                                                                 t
                                                               h
                                                              e
water back to move him forward. Thrift is his wonderful
  s
e
  c
ret; he has schooled out all extravagance. No muscle
                                                            r
                                                              i
                                                              p
ples without compensation wrist cock to heel snap to
h
i
  s
mobile mouth that siphons in the air that nurtures
                                                               h
                                                                 i
                                                             m
at half an inch above sea level so to speak.
  T
h
  e
astonishing whites of the soles of his feet rise
                                                              a
                                                              n
                                                             d
salute us on the turns. He flips, converts, and is gone
a
l
 l
in one. We watch him for signs. His arms are steady at

```
                                                                t
                                                                h
                                                                e
catch, his cadent feet tick in the stretch, they know
t
h
e
lesson well. Lungs know, too; he does not list for
                                                        a
                                                        i
                                                        r
he drives along on little sips carefully expended
b
u
t
that plum red heart pumps hard cries hurt how soon
                                                        i
                                                        t
                                                        s
near one more and makes its final surge. TIME: 4:25:9
```

Alastair Mackie

born 1925

Drappit

Believe in ghaists?

I hae tint twa yerds.
I canna mak or haud the space.
New names are aboot.
It's the auld laa, new bluid.

Last Setterday
I watched young Tamson on the baa.
He gaithers, jinks and breenges up the perk.
He sets tae the hauf, swaps pairtners syne
and Lowrie's got it joukin for the wing.
Seeven reid bobbers are showdin i the box
– it's the teuchest net in fitba thonder,
it's nickit forward lines like thrawin fish. –
But no him. Big Lowrie's throwin him a knife.
He's sneddit ane, the back's bumbazed clauchtin
air and there's the space I canna mak ava.
He hears the Roman buller o the sea,
it heists the grandstand roof and his left fit.

The goalie's like a bloke that's crucifeet
and even Jesus couldna stop that shot.
He turns awa and loups and nieves the lift
and syne they're roon 'm like wasps roon jam.

Ach, the grun's a muckle kist.
It's no canny
tae gaup on Setterday at the ghaist o ye
jiggin on the gress and you no deid.

I'll hae tae leeve wi that.

*Don't cry for Argentina for me**

It's nae o Argentina that I mind
aifter aa the play was played. (Their forwards
wi their hell-black manes wallopin the air)
Nor Brazil, passin their triangles neat
as Euclid. Na, nor ony of the goals
ootside the box, wi men haudin theirsels
and the haill line like an electric dirl.
Na. It's o Airchie Gemmill's feet steekin
a pattren on the edge o the box.
His skeely needle threidit the ba past
three men, their legs fooled by the phantom darner.
It was a baldy-heidit goblin scored the goal.
His shot, a rainbow, airches ower his name.

Christopher Logue

born 1926

Mohammed Ali

Two big blacks on a 15 bus,
Ali For King their quid pro quo:
'He may be quick – but is he strong?'
'Is Ali *strong*? O, daddy-o,
When that Mohammed pats your cheek
It breaks your little toe.'

---

*Archie Gemmill's goal for Scotland against Holland in the 1978 World Cup was considered by many to be the finest individual effort of the competition.

Charles Tomlinson
born 1927

Swimming Chenango Lake

Winter will bar the swimmer soon,
   He reads the water's autumnal hesitations
A wealth of ways: it is jarred,
   It is astir already despite its steadiness,
Where the first leaves at the first
   Tremor of the morning air have dropped
Anticipating him, launching their imprints
   Outwards in eccentric, overlapping circles.
There is a geometry of water, for this
   Squares off the cloud's redundances
And sets them floating in a nether atmosphere
   All angles and elongations: every tree
Appears a cypress as it stretches there
   And every bush that shows the season,
A shaft of fire. It is a geometry and not
   A fantasia of distorting forms, but each
Liquid variation answerable to the theme
   It makes away from, plays before:
It is a consistency, the grain of the pulsating flow.
   But he has looked long enough, and now
Body must recall the eye to its dependence
   As he scissors the waterscape apart
And sways it to tatters. Its coldness
   Holding him to itself, he grants the grasp,
For to swim is also to take hold
   On water's meaning, to move in its embrace
And to be, between grasp and grasping free.
   He reaches in-and-through to that space
The body is heir to, making a where
   In water, a possession to be relinquished
Willingly at each stroke. The image he has torn
   Flows-to behind him, healing itself,
Lifting and lengthening, splayed like the feathers
   Down an immense wing whose darkening spread
Shadows his solitariness: alone, he is unnamed
   By this baptism, where only Chenango bears a name
In a lost language he begins to construe –
   A speech of destinies and derisions, of half-
Replies to the questions his body must frame
   Frogwise across the all but penetrable element.
Human, he fronts it and, human, he draws back
   From the interior cold, the mercilessness
That yet shows a kind of mercy sustaining him.

The last sun of the year is drying his skin
Above a surface a mere mosaic of tiny shatterings,
    Where a wind is unscaping all images in the flowing obsidian,
The going-elsewhere of ripples incessantly shaping.

Philip Oakes
born 1928

Death of the Referee

A shroud, a shroud for Spring-Heeled Jack,
The only honest referee,
A crowd to keep the devil back
And sing in tune Abide with Me.

The pit unlocks its cage of doves
To tumble in the dirty air,
And far below the coffin drives
To meet the council and the mayor.

The barges drag through stiff canals,
Milky with clay and black with coal,
And as the varnished coffin falls
The mayor proclaims the grave no goal.

The colours of the local club
Flower to hide the yellow clay,
And all the foundry hammers throb
Their solace of the working day.

At home the silver trophies burn
About the mourning company,
And wishing she could be alone
The widow pours out cups of tea.

For Jack is dead, the man on springs,
Whose whistle trapped the wildest ball,
Whose portrait done in oils now hangs
For ever in the Civil Hall.

Burly with cataracts, the eyes,
Are blind at last to local fame
And friends who fail to recognise
A stranger in the golden frame.

But those who know their loss will make
The winter field his funeral,
And peel their caps to Spring-Heeled Jack
While brass bands play the March in Saul.

Iain Crichton Smith

born 1928

School Sports, at the Turnstiles

This is impossible. Though I know
(and have been told) the world's absurdity
(a dewdrop poised on nothing,
a zero
containing continually our comic seething)

and though all day wearily I've watched the flags
droop a little lower and heard money
clink at the long strides of young runners
negotiating curves in the uninteresting
way sports have, of having no ceasing,

yet suddenly I cheered as in the twilight
over the soaking ground the last came running
stretching for a prize they might not have
for more than a moment, as if somehow coming home
could be like this, a proud and hopeful yearning.

Colin Shakespeare

born 1929

To Sir Len Hutton on his 65th Birthday
June 23rd 1981

There was no violence in him, rather
The quiet mathematician
Given over to geometrics
And the study of angles,
Arcs,

Perimeters and perpendiculars,
Curves and dividing lines,
But rarely, rarely,
The parabola.

And the mystery of it all
Was the mastery of it all.

Tony Connor

born 1930

In the Locker Room

Everything's clean and jolly:
genitals, butt, and belly
show with a nakedness
that causes none distress.
Between the locker rows
heaps of abandoned clothes
lie like a beaten race
crumpled in its disgrace.
All's cheer above – the Lords
of muscle-power and words
tingling from gym and joke
relax for a quick smoke.
Glad to be back again
in this clear world of men
I banish from my mind
the dark thoughts of its kind.
I rub my itching balls:
the seed of criminals
and maniacs waits
in those hanging fruits.

Ted Hughes

born 1930

Football at Slack

Between plunging valleys, on a bareback of hill
Men in bunting colours
Bounced, and their blown ball bounced.

The blown ball jumped, and the merry-coloured men
Spouted like water to head it.
The ball blew away downwind –

The rubbery men bounced after it.
The ball jumped up and out and hung on the wind
Over a gulf of treetops.
Then they all shouted together, and the ball blew back.

Winds from fiery holes in heaven
Piled the hills darkening around them
To awe them. The glare light
Mixed its mad oils and threw glooms.
Then the rain lowered a steel press.

Hair plastered, they all just trod water
To puddle glitter. And their shouts bobbed up
Coming fine and thin, washed and happy

While the humped world sank foundering
And the valleys blued unthinkable
Under depth of Atlantic depression –

But the wingers leapt, they bicycled in air
And the goalie flew horizontal

And once again a golden holocaust
Lifted the cloud's edge, to watch them.

Martin Green

born 1932

Ode to Hackney Marshes

Twenty-two sins, said Auden, here have lease;
In our case the sin is to play badly
What the East-enders do with greater ease.

For ninety Sunday-morning minutes, sadly
Or sometimes gay, we chase the ball across
A Lowry landscape, where we swear madly

At the deaf referee, whose whistle's boss,
Trying to keep our sins within the lease
Of the white lines which make a slip a loss.

There are moments of joy; the Golden Fleece
Is putting the ball past the netless post;
A rare occurrence and a short-lived peace.

Energy we have, what we lack the most,
Skills that surge in our minds but do not show;
Our brilliant shots most often hit the post.

However the running and the swearing go
The walk back to the dressing room is like
Napoleon's retreat from burnt Moscow.

The bitterness as we approach the dike
Hangs on us like a straggling moustache
(Perhaps it's suffering we really like?).

Next Sunday we will come to Hackney Marsh
To cast our hopes upon the field of play;
The wages of twenty-two sins is harsh.

Adrian Mitchell

born 1932

World Cup Song (for the Scottish team)

    Kick that football
    Like you kick your mother
    Kick that football
    Like you kick your wife
    Kick that football
    Like you kick your children

    Footballs never kick back

J. M. Anthony

born 1934

The Last Over

Batsman batting,
Bowler bowling,
Now appealing – 'How was that?'
Umpire watching,
Quickly scotching,
'No, it did not hit the bat!'

Fine leg finer,
Cover squarer,
Six to win, one mighty clout.
Batsman sweating,
Bowler fretting,
'Will I never get him out?'

Last man facing,
Bowler racing,
'Pitch it up, don't drop one short.'
Willow crashing,
Leather flashing,
To the boundary – 'is he caught?'

Long leg hopping,
Chance of dropping
This most vital catch of all.
Fingers stinging,
Voices ringing,
Safely pouched, that leather ball.

Stephen Morris
born 1935

High Jump Poem

HIGH JUMP POEM

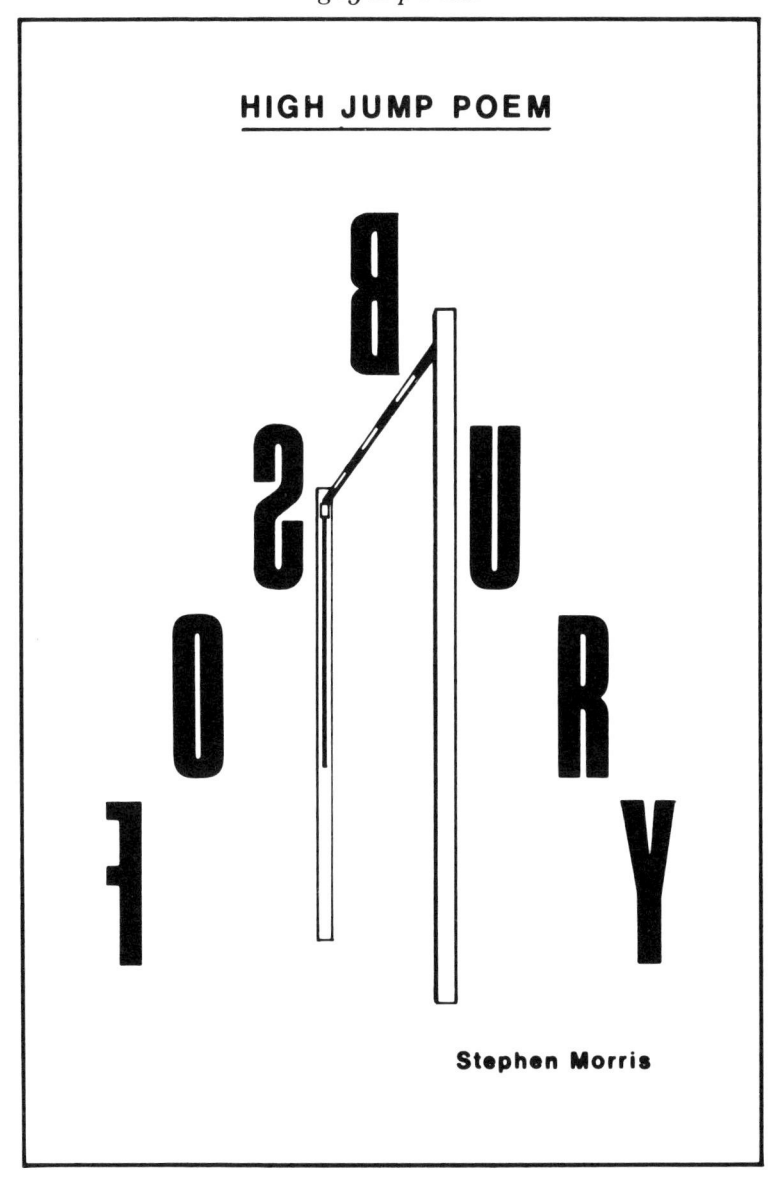

BOSFOSBURY
FOSBURY
(concrete poem arranging the letters of "FOSBURY FLOP" around a high jump bar)

Stephen Morris

Long Jump Poem

LONG JUMP POEM

RALPH BOSTON

STEPHEN MORRIS

Jeff Cloves

born 1937

Tonight I feel like a basketball hero

Tonight I feel like a basketball hero
jumping to touch the reaching boughs
of trees which hang their baskets of summer leaves
over the pavement court.
Tonight in my new white canvas boots
I am silly and pleased
for no good reason that I can think of.
Tonight I am a basketball hero
chewing gum
putting one over the Harlem Globetrotters
making all them highschool queens
winning!

*beryl and her bike**

oooh here comes beryl such a sight
for sore cyclists' eyes
trim ankles turning
blazing thighs burning up the road
and miles ahead
she shows a clean pair of wheels
to all her trailing rivals
perfect on her perfect bike
beryl always beats the clock
pure pleasure unalloyed is beryl
for beryl is the best yes
beryl is the best

beryl passes in a flash
chromey spokes italian alloy gleam
lovely clean machine flown by
in a dazzling blink
yes in the pink is beryl
for beryl is the best
and ever more shall
be so

*Beryl Burton – British best all round woman racing cyclist for the twenty-third successive year in 1981.

Fanny Blankers-Koen at Wembley*

down the years she runs and jumps
never a flying dutchman just
a truly golden girl
forever young forever first
she is the one
i remember most

For Fausto Coppi (1916−60)

When you were king of the mountains
Fausto
the kilometers hissed by
like busy moments
beneath your tyres
and the pavé was no more
than grit on your tongue
young Italian girls
threw wayside flowers
as you ticked past
spokes flashing in the sun
and in the Tour de France
peasants in the Alps
leaned from windows and shouted
'Allez Coppi!'
and forgot their own man

I remember how
you never seemed to lose
and how
you pushed your goggles
on to the brow of your thin face
and smiled as you crossed the line
and how
the photographers hounded
your lady in white
as she waited for her lean brown prince
to race
to her embrace

*where she won four gold medals in 1948

And when that dread disease
did for you
as for any mortal
I thought again of the pain
that might have been
behind the goggles and the tight grin
behind the private smile
for the waiting lady
the quiet lady in white
who waited at the line to give
the greatest prize
of all

But it's long gone now
Fausto
the flash pop picture press
the gossip column glare
has switched to another scene
you can relax
it's time to sit up in the saddle
ride on the tops
freewheel a little
you're out in front
and they'll never catch you
now

wonder boy

and so
among the traded playgound fagcards
he found his once and only heroes
and learned by heart
the minute biographies
of wingers and centre forwards
with centre partings
brilliantined hair
blue chins
knotted arms folded across
striped jerseys
clinging to manly chests
bulbous eyes fixed on the lense
of the brass and mahogany box
and the hunch-back
black-draped photographer

and so
the heroes of Wembley Albion & Hotspur
beamed their psychic messages
across the years
to the child of the forties
who dreamed
not only of Stella Coxon
who shared his pitchpine desk at school
but of Dixie Dean
and Alex James
played every night at Wembley
received the cup from the King
and was borne shoulder high
round the ground
to the sound
of brass bands and cheering crowds
and dreamed
he turned at last
to the sticky kiss of the patient Stella
who stood on tiptoe
high upon the sleepy dreamtime terraces
at every game he played
to see her wonder boy come through
and score the winning goal   always
always
in the last
minute
of
extra
time

the slow bowler's curve

downcurve the rosy ball
so slowly   slowly   slowly
indipping to the flashy blade crisp crack
sends flannelled fools in soaring fancy flight
to snatch the parted air in fear of stinging fingertips
in hope of dizzy daring price greengrazed knees is what they get
for bladesmen's lordly frozen pose announce the perfect pull
to boundary rail while railing bowler curse the field
swear to cut this cocky cracker down to size
with secret seam spell grip and spin
turn on his heel and wheel
his famous floater in

Michael Horovitz

born 1935

The Game

So . . . to the epicure stillness, stadium hush
   that succeeds the dying-down drone of corpse crush
. . . Mush of ticket touts, cub reporters, wolf-scouts
Barkers, unofficial programme louts –
Ice-cream men, hot dogs, oompah bandolineers
Motley tipsters, majorettes, gawky-gracious peers

– Solempne procession of crimsonbraid strumpeters
– Battallions of Thousands Abide with Thee
– Thousands on thousands insatiate embattled
On all sides, brightscarved, riddling berattled
Air thick inlaid with pomp of parade
   – Cameradoes connected in voice invoke
Insistent, exhorting – ill augurs, go broke!
– Strike up, kick off, wax fertile Glad Band
– Hoarse blurts, nameless contact in Oneness, ground
United through instincts closer than fog
(That caps the scene to
                dim dome of a gasworks
   – as seen from the wide berth of distant skyplanes.
   Radio plugs in and the telly explains
But it's *in*side you feel the irresistible tide
Breaking wave over wave)
                as side by side
   Onward the regnant rockers ride,
Sweep the field and subside a whole township's plush pride
Like some pregnant phalanx-unbridled steed bride
   – Delivered, relaxed – gunpowder contracting –
Apocalypse blurt
             of prescient tense heap'd-up anticipation
– One foot put wrong may mean relegation
   – OUR MAN'S HURT – bites the dirt – dread desolate cries
– Reserves cringe and tremble
                  – to quit conturbation

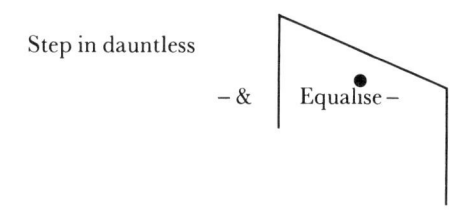

   Step in dauntless
              – &   Equalise • –

Let the news spread wiresped jubilant host

    Stop-press amplified coast to coast –
We're ahead, We're the most – Allelluia Halloo
    In unison Yoicks Huzza-yawp WE'RE THE WOLVES –

    – Steeples of choirs people Goodyear tyres,
Chubb's safety-locks & the Willenhall stocks
As Walsall-ball tunes vamp Wulfrunian runes

    . . . Wondering ear-views, Wolverine beer blues
Wulvering Heights, Villa-woof delights
    Turn again to regain – London's Orient well met
    – Nor let me forget, at Hampton yet:

Many the Hamptons drawn to play
– Hampton Wick – perfum'd garden,
    Northampton Southampton Hampton-in-Arden

    Lionel Hampton – Hampton Court – great Littlehampton
  Big **T**eaming Hampton Agonistés – Wolves
                          – Ye Pimpernel Pack Ye Glee
    – Swiftshuffling past bottomrung'd Hammers v. Pompey,
Trampoleaning the ladder the decks and the docks
Husky-galloping flashmolten socks
                        –Atalán-
                            ticking over
                            ballcrazed
                                        hoof-humdingers
      – Jets of Mullen-skrim, Jumping Jim – Finney
              Phantastickal wingers –
              Jaggery shaggery Symphony Sid
    – Sped by Billy Wright
                      – the Gridiron Sidespin Kid –

Billy
      – knight errant of 'might for right' –
Wirehaired campaign-brain Vikingshock Header –
    Albion's All-time good bloke Leader
        *Un*perfidious – terrier
                    stormtrooping bleeder . . .

Later, cuplinked laurel-balded goal-chain'd O'points meant
    He won –
              the hot seat at Highbury
    – Order of Boot   worth well muckle a ton!
    Cherouted auld wolfery
Toasting his pals with that skill-bruited loot
– Open-pampering hampers of bootfruit lopp'd full
From stalwart plum orchards ripe seasons topped

. . . Greyhound-spawned Wemblylawn'd mummer's memory sufficed
(Tho **juiced** in his gorrillorialisted cups) to store
 A new pack with devises of wolflore galore
                                             begaurrrh
   – Stern conclaves – Venerable veteran coach
   In holly and ivy league with trainers
. . . After workouts the lads lay massaged, footsore –
Warmed by his pep stalks of sage, hard-won wage
   & steaming world onion-bowl gallumphin glaze

             – as qwhan, a mere Whelp, a pup –
             Tup-kinzossled how He, Ironwrought skip
           Angelically bootskulled that entire '51 Eleven-ship
               to League-*And*-Cup's top-tip – All Heaven's trip –

   . . . But for the Arsenal's tried, & justly famed
       Reserve of hothouse power:
No wenlock of wasps zap-suction'd that flower
     – Turreted amphitheatric brawn-mower

   In fumy face of which Whirr-wolves abandoned grope
   . . . Tho every match struck spurr'd afresh
                                         the Challenge –
   To light up – flash out momently each half the finest hour
     – What use, against our red & white-hot shower! –
   Come throstle drops or shine, aye – whate'er the sky
         – Outshimmering turnstile-riot storm's eye

   Whether ball-love hove leather enginedrawn
   By mute and glory-be namelost pawn
     – Or juttingjawed thrusty ruggerbugger Punchknock
     Rolls Razorsharp- shooter – Ronnie Rooke!   – Or swart
         'Bighead' Compton – Indestructible custodian
     Of the Penalty Area Fortress – whose bell-clear kick
       Would fairground-hammer clang his brother Denis off
   Ball
       battening a crazy cricket-neck
                                   line
                                       to the cornerflag
         Thereat to pull his left leg back,
                                       & Slice the leather orb
       – Whizzing up   and – split-
                                    -secondly stock still
         At the dead shed centre of the goalmouth
                                   (just south of
                                     the totterers
     – For Doug Lishman's bonce to bounce it deftly d
   Athwart their 'keeper's   o
                     despairing   w
                          muzzlehanded   n
                                           dive –

   . . . Dream-machine of a team –
Each man a Genius, each content – for
'Modest in Victory, Cheerful in Defeat' –
       to be obscene – to be Seen I mean
       – a small but gaily gleaming cog

   Even where, in wet or midwinter season
   The bed lay rampled to a murky bog

   – Or frrosted over – hard as glacier-ramparts –
They'd brace themselves,
       Wolf Mannioned as the Nordic Middlesburghers,
  In most likewise hard and strongboned harmony –
Erect through storm,
           and failure of omened truth-to-form
– Like as if they were
Not London's gunmen grappling wild-wolves
     – Not eleven men at all
       But co-ordinated limbs of One Man
       Labouring as 'twere
              in every prime of Wife.

Roger McGough
born 1937

40 – Love

middle	aged
couple	playing
ten	nis
when	the
game	ends
and	they
go	home
the	net
will	still
be	be
tween	them

Susan Wilkins
born 1938

Running Sequence

1

    Running is a simple affirmation
the print of my shoes in the damp earth arches
over the field   is a prayer
                    my weight empties
                    into the ground
at the southwest bend I am heading for Orion
    again   again   the correspondences
       shoulders   belt   haunches of stars

2

Because the tides swing oil slicks, because the moon governs
tides and we are mostly water, we flood and ebb, blood, seed,
hunger, and at the full moon overflow, corrupt the balance.
Because the tides swing oil slicks, this generation bows
down or out not in respect, but exhaustion. Necessities
become luxuries, though for the rich it's the other way
around. I'm poor but warm because I run forward, backward,
and in circles, barking with joy.   I run.   Iran.

3

This is how I ran ten rounds of the baseball field
behind Devotion at 6 am April 17: wrists loose,
hands flapping, holding onto nothing. Whole sole
hitting the earth where new grass flames like xenon
meaning stranger or krypton meaning hidden. Sometimes the sea, the flame seem far away.
                            I try
not to crush ants' dirtcrumb hills. Robins and
grackles pulling worms scatter before me. Gulls
scream their hunger. I imagine my tide is high,
deep diver, and the sun rises in my solar plexus.
Running away. It's the running that's a way, a
moving mantra. Blessed be the sun, blessed be
the drumming of the woodpecker and the shriek of
the jay, blessed be my loneliness, blessed be the
nightshift workers returning home as the moon sets
white face in the blue west.

Anonymous

20th century

The High Jump

He slowly paced his distance off, and turned,
    Took poise, and darted forward at full speed;
Before the bar the heavy earth he spurned,
    Himself an arrow. They who saw his deed
Tensed muscles, poised and ran and leaped, and burned
    With close-drawn breath, helping him to succeed:
Now he is over, they are over, too;
Foeman and friend were flying when he flew.

Caroline Ackroyd

born 1939

Prizewinner

The ice skater
As she spins towards the end
Embodies what the trainer could not teach her;

She spins in time
Where movement's beauty seems to chime
Against another element
Not water, sky, nor mountain air
But something fathomless and clear
That holds the moment.

There is nothing human in her art
For all has been cast out
That does not thrust this pivotal ascent
One fraction further;

Springs of muscle, delicate and tough,
Impel her to the summit
She is Saturn, rings and planet;

The bracelet of her hands above the spiral
Lies on her lightly like a laurel;
Instinct steeled to pierce a barrier
Amasses speed as might a boulder

Hurtling:

Then she finds her level:
The orbit of each circle rakes the air
She will wind down but now

This potter's wheel of poetry
Isolates her where
Spoke or blade or galaxy
Cuts space chillingly.

Donald Campbell

born 1940

*Tynecastle**

I never get doun tae Tynecastle thae days
It's a guid lang while nou sen I've been
I never get doun tae Tynecastle thae days
– tho they're saying they hae a guid team
   But the team that I mind
   is the team o langsyne
when we swept aa the prizes awa
   an the boys in maroon
   were the pride o the toun
the best lads that e'er kicked a baw!
I'm thinking o Parker an Broun an Big Tam . . .
Aw, the thousands that cheered them aa on!
An my thochts haud them yet
   for I'll never forget
      My Bauld
         an My Wardbaugh
         an My Conn.

---

*Tynecastle, in Edinburgh, is the home of Heart of Midlothian FC who saw great days in the 1950s when they won the League Cup (1954) and the Cup (1956).

Robert Hughes

born 1940

The Races

Crowds assembled
Colourful scene
Jockeys mounted
Gaunt and lean
Hopeful owners
Trainers too
Tipsters punters
Ballyhoo.

Sprinters stayers
Chestnut greys
Starters orders
White flag raised
Photo finish
Objection too
Winners losers
Ballyhoo.

Pat Cutts

born 1941

Kitchen Conversation

What've you been doing, this afternoon, Son?
Rolling in mud? – Thumping a lad?
Knocking seven bells out of several lads? – I See!
(Just move over while I mash the tea!)

What were you saying? – Tell me then!
(Pass that bread over here for a minute!)
He nearly knocked your teeth out? – Why?
It's a bit much in school time, son, innit?

Was there a teacher there?
(Take your boots off the table – they're muddy!)
Yes? – Well, what did he say? –
Oh, I see! – You were playing at Rugby!!

David Morrison

born 1941

Jacqueline (Badminton)

Here's to you, Jacqueline, Jacqueline,
More power to the shuttlecock queen,
For in this light you reign supreme,
A star in the dark, my Jacqueline.

Stephen Vincent

born 1941

Basketball

I never let you come to the games. I never
invited you. You never asked. You never
saw me on the court handle the round skin
of the basketball. You never came to see me
spread my warm fingers like the edges of stars
around the ball as I went like a smooth fox
down the court my tennis shoes squeaking faster
than a grasshopper through clover. At sixteen
I travelled fast
father. Lay in, set shot, jump shot, bounce pass,
chest pass, bucking, elbowing as high as I could,
reacher for what was never given, the smooth flow
of the ball arching high towards the rim, its high arc
lifting subtly down, a smooth swish through
the star shapes of the unbroken
white net. Let me play that game again. I was on the court
with Willie, Leroy, Hobo & Sam. I the only white
with four blacks. Don't get me wrong. I was scared of them
as you of me or I of you. But it began. Somebody
poked me in the eye, it stung, and I released everything
traveling up and down the court a young man
with a quick gun and a sharp elbow. For the first time
we held together like a rapid running loom weaving
up and down between the other players who held together
stiff as strings as we broke through all their empty
edges. Suddenly it was no game. Perfect harmony
of movement and song. The referee could blow no whistle.
In victory I always refused you
entry. This time
I am going to win.

Bill Costley

born 1942

'The Smiler With The Knife' (Jeffers) — (for Peter Bates)

Social Darwinism runs amok in athletic disguise: suddenly beside
yourself, you see the runner beside you slipping a switchblade knife
    from a miniature duffelbag pouch, a hanging jury of 1 with a smile
you cannot fathom, a friendliness bordering on flirtation as common
    twilight descends, as life shared in the fast lane slackens as
you crescendo! your denouement, inescapable: trois coups de sermonce
    announcing a charade's beginning, you stumble, fall, bleed, faint,
die, are left behind the pack, are proven unfit to live, staining
    the social fabric as a statistic, simply another jogger
dyeing the flag with your unspectacular fear & misery, naively
    reddening the nylon standard. the smiler with the knife
speeds onward & upward into the pseudonymous stream, a survivor,
    a victor approaching the twilight of the bourgeois gods. perhaps
you may even have been raped, humiliated, thrown off your stride,
    yet all you communicate with the coroner is an antiseptic silence.

Douglas Dunn

born 1942

Runners

Your skin is whiter, and as you bend fat tells
Your eight years of less than Spartan marriage.
Any man can see what you have been, your legs
That too much sitting cannot discompose,
And synthesis of all movement, your running.
Men still remember you, on the last lap
Of your favourite distance, commander of championships.

Today through the hilly wood, we knew only
Lack of ease, the detritus of beauty
Left to athletes who betray their rule,
A longing of mind for its body, in which
There is no pride, or applause, and whisky
Comes back through months working against us,
The woods are smoke-filled rooms, but no one dare stop.

'In ten seconds'

In ten seconds you cannot, as marathoners do,
Think of your family, your hours of training
And everyone you know who has hopes of you.
That happens before in the nights of waiting,
Nights without sleep, or dreaming that you win,
Or dreaming that you lose, waking in sweat –
Dreams rising from your fired adrenalin –
A race you've seen which has not happened yet.
And you long to know, one way or another,
Who of all men is truly the fastest man.
In the important things, he is my brother –
In this, I'll make him look an also ran.

Muhammad Ali

born 1942

The Greatest*

This is the story about a man
With iron fists and a beautiful tan.
He talks a lot indeed,
Of a powerful punch and blinding speed.

The boxing game was slowly dying,
And fight promoters were bitterly crying
For someone somewhere to come along
With a better and different tone.

Patterson was dull, quiet and sad,
And Sonny Liston was just as bad.
Along came a kid named Cassius Clay,
Who said, 'I'll take Liston's title away.'

His athletic genius cannot be denied.
In a very short time,
He spread far and wide.

---

*Ali (then called Cassius Clay) took the World Heavyweight title from Sonny Liston with a seventh round victory on 25 February 1964; he knocked Liston out in the first round of their return match on 25 May 1965.

There's an impression you get
Watching him fight.
He plays cat and mouse,
Then turns out the light.

This colorful fighter is something to see,
And the Greatest Heavyweight Champion
I know he will be.

Feats of Clay

It all started twenty years past.
The greatest of them all was born at last.
The very first words from his Louisville lips,
'I'm pretty as a picture, and there's no one I can't whip.'
Then he said in a voice that sounded rough,
'I'm strong as an ox and twice as tough.'
The name of this Champion, I might as well say,
No other one than the greatest, Cassius Clay.
He predicts the round in which he's gonna win,
And that's the way his career has been.
He knocks them all out in the round he'll call,
And that's why he's called the Greatest of them all.

*Oscar Bonavena**

It's been a long time since I put my predictions in rhythm and rhyme,
But it was Bonavena who started it all by getting out of line.
He has asked the Commission to waive the three-knockdown rule.
He must be crazy or maybe a fool.

He couldn't have been talking to some angel from heaven,
Now he has the nerve to predict I'll fall in eleven.
If this is his joke, it's at a bad time,
For being so rash, he'll fall in Round Nine.

I understand in Argentina, the officials plainly said,
They wanted little Oscar to shave his shaggy head.
When I start going upside his heavy mop,
Bonavena will yell, 'STOP!

*In the second fight of his comeback to the ring, Ali knocked out Oscar Bonavena in the fifteenth round on 7 December 1970.

I'd rather go to the nearest barbershop.'
Before Round Nine is out,
The referee will jump and shout,
'THAT'S ALL, FOLKS, this turkey is out!'

*Joe Frazier**

I'm gonna come out smokin',
And I won't be jokin'.
I'm gonna be a peckin' and a pokin',
Pouring water on his smokin'.
It might shock you and amaze ya,
But I'm gonna destroy Joe Frazier!

The Ali—Foreman Fight†

Oh, Muhammad comes out to meet George Foreman, but George starts to retreat.
If Foreman goes back farther, he will wind up in a ringside seat.

Ali swings with a left, Ali swings with a right.
.Look at the Champ take the fight!

George keeps backing, but there's not enough room. It's a matter of time.
Now he lowers the boom. Now he lands with a right.

What a beautiful swing!
And the punch lifts George clean out of the ring.

Foreman is still rising, but the Ref wears a frown
For he can't start counting till George comes down.

Now George disappears from view. The crowd is getting frantic.
But our radar stations have picked him up. He's somewhere over the Atlantic.

Who would have thought when they came to the fight
That they would witness the launching of a black satellite?

---

*Ali had three epic battles with 'Smoking' Joe Frazier: on 8 March 1971 Ali was outpointed over fifteen rounds thus sustaining the first defeat of his professional career; he won the other two fights on points (28 January 1974) and by a technical knockout (30 September 1975).

†Ali regained the World Heavyweight title in October 1974 when he knocked out George Foreman in the eighth round.

Dave Smith

born 1942

Blues for Benny Kid Paret*

For years I've watched the corners for signs.
A hook, a jab, a feint, the peekaboo prayer of forearms,
anything for the opening, the rematch I go on dreaming.
What moves can say your life is saved?

>   As I backpedaled in a field the wasp's nest waited,
>   playing another game: a child is peeping out of
>   my eyes now, confused by the madness of stinging,
>   wave after wave rising as I tell my fists punish me,
>   counter the pain. I take my own beating and God help

>   me it hurts. Everything hurts, every punch
>   jolts, rips my ears, my cheeks, my temples. Who hurts
>   a man faster than himself? There was a wall to bounce
>   on, better than ropes. I was eleven years old.

Eleven years ago I saw the fog
turn away and rise from the welts you were
to run away with its cousin the moon. They smacked
your chest and crossed your arms because you fell down
while the aisles filled with gorgeous women, high heels
pounding like Emile, the Champion, who planted his
good two feet and stuck, stuck, stuck, stuck
until your brain tied up your tongue and sighed.

>   Somebody please, please I cried
>   make them go away, but the ball in my hand had turned
>   feverish with its crackling light. I could not let go
>   as I broke against the wall. I was eleven years old.

Benny Paret, this night in a car ferrying
my load of darkness like a ring no one escapes,
I am bobbing and weaving in fog split only by a radio
whose harsh gargle is eleven years old, a voice in the air

telling the night you are down, counting time,
and I hear other voices from corners with bad moves say
Get up, you son of a bitch, get up! But you will not
get up again in my life where the only sign you give me

---

*Bennie Paret died ten days after being defeated by Emile Griffith in a welterweight contest on 24 March 1963 at Madison Square Gardens.

is a moon I remember sailing down on your heart
and blood growing wings to fly up in your eyes.
And there, there the punches no one feels grow weak,
as the wall looms, break through the best prayer you had
to dump you dizzied and dreaming in the green grass.

Alan Bold

born 1943

Game and Match

Like Gods kicking a world about
The players flail at the ball.
Their brains are in their feet,
Their single mind is fixed on goal.

'Come in number six, your time's up'
Shouts a florid face in the crowd.
The player dreams of a golden cup,
Its grail-like glitters gleam in his head.

Meanwhile, there's a match to be won
And the boot will have to be put in;
'It's a man's game, football, son,
And there's a man's way to win.'

And later the bruised losers reflect
In the light of the setting sun
That they lost but kept their self-respect
While the winners merely won.

Kenny Dalglish

In a blinding flash
Of speed Dalglish
Is on the ball:
A player with all
The skills, a stunner,
A glorious match-winner
Who can make midfield space
Before using his pace
To come and score

Then bask in the roar
Of the crowd, arms in the air.
He could play anywhere
For, intensely creative
And imaginative,
His athletic mind seems to know
Exactly where the ball should go
And at the end
Of a buildup, his blend
Of strength, agility,
Natural ability,
Flawless ball-controls
Make unforgettable goals
From a volley, a side-kick,
A graceful leaping headflick:
Subtle, supple, cunning, quick
Dalglish, sheer football magic.

Archie Gemmill

Metaphor-mongers talk of terriers
When they want to suggest tenacity
As a Scottish quality
But I think somehow
The spirit of the tiger
Has entered this man
And made him awesome
In his grip on the game
For he eats up attackers
Then leaps into attack himself
Then tears back ferociously
To bring down any threat
In Scotland's territory.
He has the old bright flame, the fire
That Billy Bremner
Once carried as a torch for Scotland,
The same will to win,
To get stuck-in,
The same total
Gift of giving all
And then some more.
Physically quite small
He is compact,
Wiry and tough –
In fact
The great wee Scotsman
Writ very large.

The Swimmer

He clings to the water, cleaves
It to him then kicks and shoves
The wet around him, heaves
His chest and shoulders, moves
Into an old dimension.
His instincts take over,
He achieves suspension
In a space full of forever,
A place familiar as a stone's splash
Into a running river
Or a wave's cautious crash
On the edge
Of a sunset-sucking ocean.
Now he's in another age,
Blows bubbles underwater
And watches the air
Take a shine to itself, so clear
It seems to clean the atmosphere.
He shakes himself, lashes out
And presses on
Now that the game's afoot.
He swims, he's having fun
Fancying himself, without a fin,
As a boy becoming dolphin;
Seeing himself take first place
In an inhuman race.
Still, that's a myth,
An aspect of the truth
That hardly touches this liquid moment
That finds him in his element.

The Cyclist

Every morning I see him pedalling past
And wonder what the hell he's doing.
He seems to be getting nowhere fast;
He's always there, fro-ing and to-ing.

It's not so much an art as a skill;
This method of using the old wheel.
The cyclist negotiates a grim hill
Sitting on a tubular triangle of steel.

What's the point? Where's he going?
Just somewhere away from here.
So he goes through the motions, slowing
Briefly as he changes gear.

There's pain in his face as he accelerates,
Relief as he slowly slows down,
Impatience as he stops and waits
While the traffic lights conduct the town.

Still, he's out and about out there:
That's his religious function.
Bless him with a blue gust of warm air,
Not mincing piety, not extreme unction.

Bruce Davies

born 1943

The Rugby Match

The hour has arrived, the battle dress is donned with pride
The captain beats his vocal drum
Hormones secrete, oily hands massage the flesh.
Pungent odour smarts the eye
Muscles flex, the gurgling stomach rolls
Friend becomes the faceless foe
The glinting stud upon the boot becomes a flash,
As simulated glory is conjured on the spot.
The chanting crowd are echoes in the numbed mind
The pulses race from hollow, empty hearts
The taped, greased giants wide and tall
Snort and bite upon the plastic bit
Gnarled, battered faces of so many such an hour
The doors open, the cold air cools the cold sweat,
The skin pimples, the hairs bristle
The body shivers, the minute has arrived.
From darkness to the light of day
The chanting crowd are haloed by the cloudy blue
Clatter over the concrete muffled by the beckoning green.
Whitened iron, majestic to the eye
Spacial zones of joy and anguish
Intriguingly omnipotent to the victor's laurels.
Leather lofted high, the ritual begins.
Gladiatorial mass awaits, strong arms bind the sturdy hip
Head to head the bodies crunch and fall,

Heaving hearts and driving legs
Bloodied nose, eyes with blackened blush
Disciplined protection thwarts the foe
Ball awaits; the gilted edge
From power to the speed of limb; the fleet of foot
The ball caressed with guise and guile
The stride has changed, the limbs evade the grasping hands
To glory with the leather.
The chanting crowd with love and hatred
The bouncing leather tantalizes aching limbs;
Frustrates the tired thoughts.
The spirit never wanes, muscle bends the bone.
Power, pain, pleasure are sensitized with time and space.
The whistle shrieks, elation, depression,
The victors, the vanquished
The shrug, the smile, the clasp of fraternity
The rugby match.

Tom Leonard

born 1944

*Yon Night**

yonwuz sum night
thi Leeds gemmit Hamdin
a hunnirn thurty four thousan
aw singing
yilnivir wok alone

wee burdnma wurk then
nutsnur a wuz
but she wuzny intristid
yi no thi wey

well there wuzza stonnin
ana wuz thaht happy
ana wuz thaht fed up
hoffa mi wuz greetnaboot Celtic
anhoffa mi wuz greetnaboot hur

big wain thata wuz
a kin laffitit noo

---

*In the semi-final of the 1970 European Cup, Celtic defeated Leeds United in what was billed as the Battle of Britain. At Leeds, Celtic won 0–1; at Hampden, Bremner scored first for Leeds then Hughes and Murdoch put Celtic ahead.

Fireworks*

up cumzthi wee man
beats three men
slingzowra crackir

an Lennux
aw yi wahntia seenim
coolizza queue cumbir

bump
rightnthi riggin
poastij stamp
a rockit

that wuzzit
that wuzthi end

finisht

from *Unrelated Incidents*

sittn guzz
lin a can
a newcastle
brown wotchin
scotsport hum
min thi furst
movement a
nielsen's thurd
symphony happy
iz larry yi
might say;

a wuz jist turn
in ovir thi
possibility uv
oapnin anuthir
can whin thi
centre forward
picked up
a loose baw:
hi huddiz back

---

*Celtic's winger Jimmy Johnstone was known as the 'wee man'; like team-mate Bobby Lennox he had an appetite for attacking football.

tay thi
right back iz
hi caught
it wayiz in-
step n jist
faintn this way
then that
way, hi turnd
n cracked it;
aw anwan move-
ment; in ti
thi net.

Danny Pollock

born 1944

Goalkeeper's Lament

Pass the ball
over here
Pass the ball
over here

Down the field
down the wing
carried on a roar
as supporters sing

A wasted chance
that I could see
why didn't you pass
the ball to me?

It's my turn,
I want a kick
I want the crowd to shout my name
Their defence
will look so sick
Who said football's 'just a game'?

I'm a goalkeeper
I hate this role
Pass the ball –
I'll score a goal!

Dart Board Dave

I know,
it's been said before,
I ain't exactly slim!
I've been called
'a tub of lard',
and that's just to begin!

But deep inside this portly frame
looking far from neat,
lurks a natural athlete
that's never known defeat.

My game is darts
I'm an ace
my aim is straight and true
My hand is steady
as a rock,
my eyes are cool ice blue.

The room is dark and silent
everyone sits still
as I move in like a panther
ready for the kill.

I lay down my cigarette
I take a drink of beer
easing off the tension
as victory creeps near.

Double-top is needed
I have just one shot,
my dart is radar-guided
as it hits the spot.

Seb Coe eat your heart out
'cause you could be like me
Smoking fags and drinking beer
and tasting sweet victory.

Peter Bond

born 1945

Pockets of Resistance*

'Life is a game of snooker,'
The sage of South Africa said.
'To start with, the table's too crowded,
So first, you get rid of the Reds.
Then you can go for the Coloureds.
Knock them all clean out of sight
But save your best whack
To put down the Black
Until all that's left is the white.'

Martin Hall

born 1945

I'll Stand the Lot of You

I'll stand the lot of you, I said
to the other kids. They said: Right!

I was Wolves 1957–58:
Finlayson; Stuart, Harris; Slater, Wright, Flowers;
Deeley, Broadbent, Murray, Mason, Mullen.
The other kids were Rest of the World:
Banks; Pele, Best; Best, Pele, Pele;
Best, Pele, Charlton, Pele, Best.
Jimmy Murray kicked off for Wolves.

Wolves were well on top in the opening minutes,
then Rest of the World broke away and scored
seven lucky goals. Wolves were in trouble!
But then tragedy struck Rest of the World:
Pele had to go and do their homework!
They were soon followed by Best and Charlton.
It was Wolves versus Banks!
Now Wolves played like a man possessed.
Soon they were on level terms!

---

 y of the leading snooker professionals play in South Africa during the winter.

Seven-all, and only minutes to go,
when suddenly – sensation! Banks went off
to watch the Cup Final on television!
Seconds later, a pinpoint Mullen centre
found Peter Broadbent completely unmarked
in front of goal. What a chance!

He missed it,
and Wolves trooped sadly off towards their bike.

John Whitworth

born 1945

Sporting Prints

i. For A Young Athlete

Written in the seventeenth-century style on the occasion of David Gower's first Test century, against New Zealand at The Oval in July 1978.

We honour him because
He is young, and all he does
Partakes of youthfulness,
Simplicity and grace.
In the old time, they say
Venus kept away
From Hades' iron rede
Pretty Ganymede
Who measured wine to Jove
And touched the Queen of Love
With human sorrow, long
Ago when the Earth was young.

ii. Tinned Strawberries

A Wimbledon late sky like streaky bacon
    As the last Brit dies on Centre. Out on 3
Wendy Turnbull and six-gun Riessen take on
    Old stoneface Tony Roche and Miss Bunge,
Intent and pink and fair. Roche's backhand,
    Still zonking nicely, raises clouds of dust.
A Corporation cart digests a sack and
    Roche pauses, grunts, 'They've come for me at last,'

Then flattens Wendy with a skidding bounce.
   How pretty tennis is, how instantly
Forgettable. I saw Lew Hoad once
   In ten inch quavering black and white. *Who's he?*
Riessen applauds. Roche and Miss Bunge win.
The autograph collectors amble in.

Slow Left Arm

Cricket's a lot like love on the whole – it
   Tastes of sweet damn all
And a beautiful, boring afternoon
Waiting for something to happen soon.
Christopher Morrison takes the ball
   And calls me up to bowl it.

Every lover must have his day
   And this is the day for me.
Three clean bowled, two leg before,
Christopher Morrison stumps one more.
Last man in's a hitter – he
   Might make a little hay.

But cow-shot corner sees him caught.
   Seven for twenty-four!
O kiss me, remember me, nymph in thy orisons!
Jammy young sod, murmurs Christopher Morrison.
What the lads want is lots lots more
   Old films and bloody sport.

Peter Forbes

born 1947

Cricket

The world's as sly as a salesman's spiel,
Problems loom like clotted clouds,
And we pray for rain and the absence of blight,
Living tight-fisted, hand-to-mouth,
Snatching at scraps of fact and fancy,
Intuition, hearsay, dogma and doubt.

So in this twittering twilight zone,
Between one childhood and the next,
To square up now to the leather ball
Seems one firm deed in a shifty world –
It'll bruise your body or smash your stumps,
So middle *this* if nothing else;
It could be your only chance
To hit one smack between the eyes:
Unsubtle, square, and unlike life.

Building an Innings

I need runs behind not ahead of my name,
You're not in till you're half-way through in this game.

Always the terror unknown to old hands,
Dreading one-hit wonders and one-night stands.

Always the fear of inviting my fate,
Playing too soon or playing too late.

Impatient to be in the ripe middle span,
The fifties behind and a hundred to plan.

Always those queasy moments at the start,
Loving and loathing the *poésie de depart*.

Now you know why I panicked when you said no.
I thought I was in for a lifetime or so.

Alan Frost

born 1947

Goal!

Goal!
    At that time he forgot
    The miseries of home, the creditors
    The going bald, the anodyne slavery

Goal!
    At that moment he rose
    In vicarious triumph from the humdrum
    Of nothing life, of zero significance

Goal!
> At that moment he danced
> Wildly like a kid with the random carnival
> Of touchpaper delinquescents on the terrace

Goal!
> At that moment the simple bulge
> Of a white leather orb in a cage of netting
> Could erupt such ecstasy in his being

Goal!
> At that moment a dream lived
> Countless surreal desires were expiated
> A hosanna phalanx of arms proclaimed

Goal!
> At that moment his heart jumped
> An evanescent climax freed him
> From the anchor of everyday thought

Goal!
> At that moment he scaled
> The apex of life
> For at that moment – he was happy

Goal!

Car

> I am an agent of death
> Beware me
> Though I respond to your impatient feet
> And grind my teeth
> At your ham-fisted gear-change
> Think me not a faithful slave
> Do not mistake patience for servitude
> Beware me –
> > I am an agent of *death*

> I am a Jezebel of steel
> Desire me
> For I respond to your pulsating drives
> And flash my torso
> Through your urban armadas
> Think of me as seductive
> Purring as you lapse into fantasy
> Desire me –
> > I am a Jezebel of *death*

I am a symbol of wealth
Worship me
For I respond to your pagan desires
And turn men's heads
Through your screaming manoeuvres
Think of me as impressive
Catching women's eyes for your vanity
Worship me –
    I am a symbol of *wealth*

I am a rusting heap of scrap
Abuse me
For I respond to your depressing needs
And serve my driver
Through your tedious routines
Think of me as expensive
Breaking down but vital to your functions
Abuse me –
    I am a rusting heap of *scrap*

I am an agent of death
Beware me
Though I respond to your various feet
And show my worth
At your arrogant demands
Think me not a faultless thing
Do not mistake safety for synthesis
Beware me –
    I am an agent of *death*

Ron Butlin

born 1949

*Football Fantasy: Argentina 1978**

A ship lies gasping in the cupboard:
its crew disturbs my sleep night after night
with their demands to put to sea.

– But no sooner do I close my eyes
and start imagining to myself the long ball
from Bruce Rioch that I take past one man, side-
flick past a second and am lining up for a Peter Lorimer-

---

*when Scotland, captained by Bruce Rioch, qualified for the World Cup and (despite the talents of Lorimer and others) were eliminated after two disastrous matches against Peru and Iran and one victory over Holland.

rocket-postage-stamp in the top right hand corner
while the crowd goes wild, wild, wild
— when from behind the terraces I hear the opening strains
of the first of that evening's many sea-shanties.

I try to ignore it, and tell myself that back home
all Scotland's sitting boozed and bunnetted in front of the TV,
watching me with only the goalie to beat
and the World Cup as good as on the mantlepiece.

— But already the crowd's been infiltrated;
already some of them
(I suspect the ones with eye-patches,
and anchors over their shoulders)
have started singing 'Hearts of Oak'
in counterpoint to the crowd's roar
— and I see the goal-posts and netting sway gently
in an easterly breeze.

I try to ignore it for the ball's still at my feet
and I tell myself that back home
all Scotland's standing on the sofas and the sideboards
cheering themselves tartan.

— But already the Easterly has freshened up
and the goal-posts are listing slightly
and, as the netting billows, are pulling away from the terraces
where *everyone's* now wearing an eye-patch
and has an anchor over his shoulder
— some of them are even watching the game through telescopes!

I try to ignore them and line up the ball for the big one,
the one that's going to be the one and only,
the most beautiful thing to come out of Scotland
since McEwan's Export,
the one they'll action-replay till the film falls apart.

The crowd gives out with 'Steady boys, steady!'
I try to ignore it
— the ball turns into a pink bobbing marker-buoy!
I try to ignore it
— the goals are towing the terraces of shantying sailors
out to sea!
I try to ignore it:
Scotland's not going to be robbed, not this time!

Then suddenly I am alone in Argentina.
No crowd, no ball, no goals, no cup.
The grass is turning to sea-water
— and it's a long swim home!

Christopher Reid

born 1949

Folk Tale

And then there was a mad astronomer,
the shepherd of a solitary moon,
who chased his tiny, pock-marked planet
over the hills for half a morning.

The countryside was his enemy:
uncouth heather and highwayman copses
kept taking his jewel and hiding it.
His only friends were the eighteen pickpockets.

Once he ambled into a nostril
of sand, that sneezed and sneezed to expel him.
He left wounds on grassy pelts
and green tonsures. He often drew mud.

From time to time, coming upon
the moon, diffident, snug as a mushroom
on dank turf, he'd take his club
and smack it back into the sky.

It must have had occult properties,
to have led him so gullibly over the hills
in his houndstooth cap and tweed knickerbockers,
feinting vague arcs in the moist air.

Baldanders

Pity the poor weightlifter
alone on his catasta,

who carries his pregnant belly
in the hammock of his leotard

like a melon wedged in a shopping-bag . . .
A volatile prima donna,

he flaps his fingernails dry,
then – squat as an armchair –

gropes about the floor
for inspiration, and finds it there.

His Japanese muscularity
resolves to domestic parody.

Glazed, like a mantelpiece frog,
he strains to become

the World Champion (somebody, answer it!)
Human Telephone.

Carlton C. Allen

born 1954

Wimbledon Wizard

Centre Court
Crowd begins
A racket of applause
For the prince's game
Knowing
A scorched missile
Plays final serve

The verve of the genius
Envelopes
The arena

He is known
to Victory
He jumps delightedly

Whoosh
A wizard
feted in deliverance

Winging towards
Idolation

*Platinum Ballerina**

No 7
Flashes by
The Revs
   Fly
    High
With a Platinum rider

    Active
    Brilliant
A gifted BALLERINA
    On Sun Kissed Wheels
     Kicking the heels
      of Rivals
     Made of lesser steels

    Running together
    Hell for leather
The engine sings
   A staccato bark

Awaking Motorcycle Angels

     Who Pray,

High above the Park
One wave's the Chequered Flag

   To Greet
    FIRST
   Across the glory line
    SAFE
   Victorious

Showing a Radiant face
   Acknowledging his place
    First in seasons
        of time.

*Barry Sheene at Donington Park circuit.

F. Scott Monument

born 1956

The Keepfit Fiend

He checks his calories against a chart.
He's had his limit, knows what's good for him.
Now a lively saunter to the gym
Where keeping fit is something of an art.

He does four pressups, then he starts to sweat.
He skips a bit, he sweats a little more.
He feels the sweat and blesses every pore:
The taste of sweat is exquisitely sweet.

He won't admit it's getting rather late
To reproduce the youth he knows he's lost.
He's trying hard to win – at what a cost –
Now that he's overdrawn and overweight.

He saves his breath; himself he cannot save.
His fitness fad puts one fit in the grave.

The Dartist

He watches Eric Bristow on the box
And sees the treble twenties darting home.
He knows he's set to make his local team:
He also serves who only stands and chalks.

His moment comes, the tournament begins:
It's treble this, it's double this and that.
His pinkie's poised, he's looking really great,
He pushes home the darts like drawing pins.

His life has changed, his nights out with the lads
Are magic – he's heroic in their eyes.
He packs his job in for a higher prize:
His walls are weakened by a zillion thuds.

When his wife leaves he shrugs and shakes his head.
He much prefers to score three-in-a-bed.

The Angler

Now here's a nutter who looks dressed to thrill
With rubber gear, a rod and thigh-high boots;
He comes equipped with maggots, flies and floats
And licks his lips and thinks about the kill.

His cold blood-sport's an open secret, though:
Like other addicts he is hooked on death.
His fishing, when you strip away the myth,
Is one man's torture of an easy prey.

His sado-masochism is pronounced:
He moans about the weather and the wet
Yet stands hip-deep in water with a net
Thinking of the little fish he's trounced.

He's cold and, when he turns up to his club,
He looks like something from a marble slab.

The Hillwalker

He thinks of Scotland, there beneath his feet,
As almost human, like the human race;
And so he treads this almost human face,
Confers on it the Order of the Boot.

The hills seduce him just by being there:
Their contours swell, his willing body soars.
His wife's a martyr to the Great Outdoors
And wonders what he does in the fresh air.

If she could see him now she'd change her tune:
His face is flushed, his breath comes out in gulps.
It's true he's on the slopes and not the Alps
But that's almost enough to make him swoon.

The climax of his climb's its own reward:
He'll sleep when he gets home tonight, dog-tired.

The Golf Freak

He's not a clown, he's just attired for golf –
All kitted out in cap and shiny shoes.
He's bought the lot, the compleat golfer shows
He's lost his inhibitions, found himself.

This one's so proper in his place of work,
A pinstripe-suited safe conservative.
Come Saturday he's up and full of drive
Way out there swinging hard from dawn to dark.

His wife and kids have labelled him a sap
But he knows different, feels he has some style,
And as he cuts up rough reveals his skill:
His body is his only handicap.

He's glad now he's a convert to the game:
Without a club (and balls) life's rather tame.

Acknowledgements

In shaping this anthology I have been greatly aided and abetted by two enthusiasts: Craig Sharp of Birmingham University's Department of Physical Education; and my American friend Bill Costley. To both of them I am most grateful for making constructive suggestions and obtaining texts. Every effort has been made to contact copyright holders; in the event of an inadvertent omission I should be notified and can be contacted via Mainstream Publishing. For permission to reproduce poems in this anthology acknowledgement is made as follows:

Dannie Abse for a poem from *Collected Poems 1948–1976* (Hutchinson) by permission of the Author.
Caroline Ackroyd by permission of the Author.
Carlton C. Allen by permission of the Author.
Kenneth Allott by permission of Miriam Allott.
J. M. Anthony by permission of the Author.
John Arlott by permission of the Author.
John Betjeman for a poem from *Collected Poems* by permission of the Author and John Murray (Publishers) Ltd.
Alan Bold by permission of the Author.
Peter Bond by permission of the Author.
Ron Butlin by permission of the Author.
Donald Campbell by permission of the Author.
Jeff Cloves by permission of the Author.
Tony Connor by permission of the Author.
Bill Costley by permission of the Author.
Pat Cutts by permission of the Author.
Bruce Davies by permission of the Author.
Douglas Dunn for 'Runners' from *The Happier Life* by permission of the Author and Faber and Faber Ltd; for 'In ten seconds' from the film *Athletes* (BBC1) by permission of the Author.
Gavin Ewart for a poem from *Or Where A Young Penguin Lies Screaming* (Gollancz) by permission of the Author.
F. Scott Fitzgerald for a poem from *Poems 1911–1940* (Bruccoli Clark), ed. Matthew J. Bruccoli, by permission of Matthew J. Bruccoli.
Peter Forbes for 'Cricket' from *The Aerial Noctiluca* by permission of Poet and Printer; for 'Building an Innings' by permission of the Author.
Alan Frost by permission of the Author.
Walker Gibson for a poem from *The Reckless Spenders* (Indiana University Press) by permission of the Author.
Martin Green by permission of the Author.
Martin Hall by permission of the Author.
Michael Horovitz for Book VI of *The Wolverhampton Wanderer* (Latimer New Dimension) by permission of the Author.
A. E. Housman for a poem from *Collected Poems* by permission of Jonathan Cape Ltd and the Society of Authors as the literary representative of the Estate of A. E. Housman.
Ted Hughes for a poem from *Remains of Elmet* by permission of Faber and Faber Ltd.
Robert Hughes by permission of the Author.

Michael Ivens by permission of the Author.
John Jarvis by permission of the Author.
James Kirkup by permission of the Author.
Kenneth Koch by permission of the Author.
Maxine Kumin by permission of the Author.
Tom Leonard for poems from *Intimate Voices* by permission of the Author.
Christopher Logue for a poem from *Ode to the Dodo, Poems 1953 to 1978* (Jonathan Cape) by permission of the Author.
Norman MacCaig by permission of the Author.
Hugh MacDiarmid by permission of Valda Grieve for the Estate of Hugh MacDiarmid.
Roger McGough for a poem from *After the Merrymaking* (Jonathan Cape) by permission of A. D. Peters and Co Ltd.
Alastair Mackie by permission of the Author.
Louis MacNeice for a poem from *The Collected Poems of Louis MacNeice* by permission of Faber and Faber Ltd.
John Masefield by permission of the Society of Authors as the literary representative of the Estate of John Masefield.
Adrian Mitchell for a poem from *For Beauty Douglas: Collected Poems 1953—79* (Allison and Busby) by permission of the Author.
F. Scott Monument by permission of the Author.
Stephen Morris by permission of the Author.
David Morrison by permission of the Author.
Sir Henry Newbolt for a poem from *Selected Poems by Henry Newbolt* by permission of Peter Newbolt.
Norman Nicholson for a poem from *A Local Habitation* (Faber and Faber) by permission of David Higham Associates Ltd.
Alfred Noyes by permission of the Trustees of the Alfred Noyes Estate.
Philip Oakes by permission of the Author.
Eugene O'Neil for a poem from *Poems 1912—44*, edited by Donald Gallup, by permission of the Executors of the Eugene O'Neill Estate, Donald Gallup and Jonathan Cape Ltd.
Betty Parvin by permission of the Author.
Danny Pollock by permission of the Author.
Ezra Pound for a poem from *Collected Shorter Poems* by permission of Faber and Faber Ltd.
Christopher Reid for 'Baldanders' from *Arcadia* and 'Folk Tale' from *Pea Soup* by permission of the Author and Oxford University Press.
Alan Ross by permission of the Author.
Siegfried Sassoon by permission of George Sassoon.
Vernon Scannell by permission of the Author.
Robert Service by permission of Feinman and Krasilovsky, P.C.
Colin Shakespeare by permission of the Author.
Dave Smith for a poem from *Cumberland Station* by permission of the Author and University of Illinois press.
Iain Crichton Smith by permission of the Author.
John Smith for a poem from *A Landscape of My Own* (Robson Books) by permission of the Author.
J. C. Squire for a poem from *Collected Poems* by permission of Macmillan, London and Basingstoke.
Charles Tomlinson by permission of the Author.
Stephen Vincent for a poem from *White Lights & Whale Hearts* (The Crossing Press) by permission of the Author.
John Whitworth by permission of the Author.

Susan Wilkins by permission of the Author.
Frederick J. Willis by permission of the Author.
P. G. Wodehouse by permission of Lady Ethel Wodehouse.
W. B. Yeats for a poem from *The Collected Poems of W. B. Yeats* by permission of Michael B. Yeats, Anne Yeats and Macmillan London Ltd.

Glossary

antrin, strange

bauld, bold
besom, broom
birkie, youth
bonspeil, curling contest
breenge, rush
brig, bridge
buller, gurgle
bumbaze, confound

ca', drive
callant, lad
carl, man
cauldrife, chilly
channel stane, curling stone
chield, fellow
claucht, clutch
coof, fool
craw, crow
creel, confusion
crokonition, destruction
cronach, dirge
crouse, lively

deoch-an-dorras, parting glass
dule, goal

fash, care
fasheous, troublesome
fleeched, pled
fyke, fidget

ghaists, ghosts
grane, groan
grun, ground

heist, lift
howf, place
hunkers, squatting with hams near heels

ilk, each
ilka, every

kist, coffin
kittle, difficult

lave, remainder
lift, sky
limmer, rascal
lith, joint
loup, leap

marrow, equal
mott, mound
moudiewarp, mole
muckle, large

nieve, punch

pow, head

row, roll
rowth, plenty

scaith, loss
skip, captain of a rink
skite, skid
sned, prune
soop, sweep
stirk, a cattle beast
swack, supple

teind, stipend
teuch, tough
thrang, throng
tint, lost
trauchle, draggle

unco, very

warsle, wrestle
wean, child
whazzle, wheeze
win awa', get away

Index of Poets

Abse, Danny	132-3	Lefroy, Edward Cracroft	83
Ackroyd, Caroline	166-7	Leonard, Tom	179-81
Ali, Muhammad	171-3	Logue, Christopher	149
Allen, Carlton C.	191-2	Love, James	10-17
Allot, Kenneth	120-1	MacCaig, Norman	119
Arlott, John	121-2	MacDiarmid, Hugh	111-3
Anthony, J. M.	154	McGough, Roger	166
Betjamin, Sir John	116	Mackie, Alistair	146-7
Bold, Alan	175-8	MacNeice, Louis	117
Bond, Peter	183	Masefield, John	97-8
Booth, Philip	135	Mitchell, Adrian	155
Bultin, Ron	188-9	Monument, F. Scott	193-5
Byron, Lord George Gordon	47-8	Moore, Thomas	26-7
Campbell, Donald	167	Morris, Stephen	155-6
Carroll, Lewis	61	Morrison, David	169
Cloves, Jeff	157-60	Murray, George	59
Coleridge, Samuel Taylor	22	Newbolt, Sir Henry	94-5
Collins, Rev. Emanuel	9	Nicholson, Norman	122
Connor, Tony	151	Noyes, Alfred	98-9
Costley, Bill	170	Oakes, Philip	149-50
Crane, Hart	115-6	O'Neill, Eugene	110-11
Crane, Stephen	96	Parvin, Betty	123
Cutts, Pat	168	Pollock, Danny	181-2
Davies, Bruce	178-9	Pound, Ezra	109
Doyle, Arthur Conan	86-8	Pudney, John	118
Drummond, William Henry	80-3	Ramsey, Allan	7-9
Dunn, Douglas	170-1	Reid, Christopher	190-1
Ewart, Gavin	124	Reynolds, J. H.	50-55
Fitzgerald, F. Scott	114	Ross, Alan	129-31
Forbes, Peter	185-6	Sassoon, Siegfried	110
Frost, Alan	186-8	Scannell, Vernon	128
Gibson, Walker	127	Service, Robert	96-7
Grace, G. F.	78	Shakespeare, Colin	150-1
Grahame, James	18	Sharp, William	84-6
Green, Martin	152-3	Smith, Dave	174-5
Gregson, Bob	25-6	Smith, Iain Crichton	150
Hall, Martin	183-4	Smith, John	134
Hazel, Tom	29-30	Sorley, Charles Hamilton	113
Hemans, Felicia	48-9	Spencer, Bernard	118
Higgins, F. R.	115	Squire, J. C.	102-8
Hogg, James	19	Stephen, J. K.	89-93
Horovitz, Michael	161-4	Stevenson, Robert Louis	79
Houseman, A. E.	88-9	Swinburne, Algernon Charles	62-5
Hughes, Robert	168	Tomlinson, Charles	148-9
Hughes, Ted	151-2	Thompson, Francis	93-4
Ivens, Michael	134	Vincent, Stephen	169
Jarvis, John	126-7	Whitman, Walt	60
Keats, John	56	Whitworth, John	184-5
Kennedy, James	70-7	Wilkins, Susan	165
Kircup, James	133	Williams, William Carlos	100-1
Koch, Kenneth	136-44	Willis, Jake	125
Kumin, Maxine	145-6	Wodehouse, P. G.	99-100
Lang, Andrew	65-9	Wordsworth, William	22
Lawson, Frederick	23-5	Yeats, W. B.	95